THE CUBAN FIVE talk about their lives
within the US working class

"It's the poor who face the savagery
of the US 'justice' system"

is series

ALICE WATERS

THE CUBAN FIVE talk about their lives
within the US working class

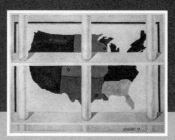

"It's the poor who face
the savagery of the
US 'justice' system"

Pathfinder
New York   London   Montreal   Sydney

Edited by Mary-Alice Waters

Copyright © 2016 by Pathfinder Press

ISBN 978-1-60488-085-4
Library of Congress control number 2015960266
Manufactured in Canada

First edition, 2016
Second printing, 2016

COVER DESIGN: Toni Gorton
ABOUT THE COVER PAINTING:

Five Distant Prisons by Antonio Guerrero
"They chose five distant points for us to serve our unjust sentences: Gerardo to California. Ramón to Texas. René to Pennsylvania. Fernando to Wisconsin. Me to Colorado. . . . Nothing, however, could stop the Five from continuing to act as one. Nothing could keep us from receiving messages from hundreds of friends around the world. Nothing could prevent us from marching together with our people and all our supporters in the long battle for justice and freedom." —ANTONIO GUERRERO, AUGUST 2014

Pathfinder
www.pathfinderpress.com
E-mail: pathfinder@pathfinderpress.com

CONTENTS

**WE WILL TAKE OUR PLACE IN THE TRENCHES
AND BE JUDGED BY THE WORK WE DO**

Photographs and illustrations

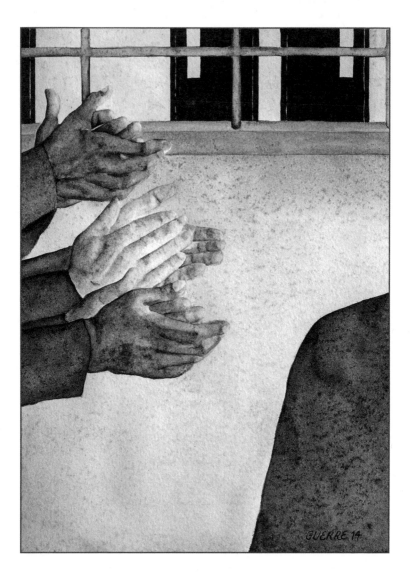

The Jury's Verdict, watercolor by Antonio Guerrero.

"On June 8, 2001, after the jury found us guilty of all charges, we returned late that day to prison. To our great surprise, when we arrived we were greeted with loud applause from the big majority of those we had been living alongside during the months of the trial.... It was what might truly be called the first act of solidarity with our case." —*Antonio Guerrero*

Introduction

BY MARY-ALICE WATERS

Nothing that happened is about us as individuals.
It's about the Cuban people who we represent.

ANTONIO GUERRERO
FEBRUARY 2015

On September 12, 1998, in "shock and awe" predawn raids by the Clinton administration's federal police force, the US government arrested ten Cubans living and working in south Florida and announced to the world that they had captured a network of "Castro's spies." Five of those arrested rapidly cut deals to collaborate with their jailers and disappeared from history.

The other five from that moment on began writing a new chapter in the history of the Cuban Revolution. A new chapter in the struggle of the international working class and popular masses to free themselves from imperialist oppression and capitalist exploitation.

Gerardo Hernández, Ramón Labañino, Antonio Guerrero, Fernando González, and René González are today known around the world as the Cuban Five, and in Cuba as the Five Heroes.

In face of intense pressure from Washington's prosecutors, each of the Five refused to turn traitor to themselves and the revolution they were defending. They spurned threats, enticements, and banishment to seventeen months in the hole. They refused to plead guilty to frame-up charges hurled against them by the US government or "plea bargain" with their prosecutors. They proudly defended the work they were doing to protect their people against terrorist attacks launched with impunity from US soil by Cuban enemies of the revolution—explaining how and why their actions were in the interests of the vast majority of the American people, as well.

With unbroken dignity and confidence, the Five faced the full "savagery" of the capitalist justice system they describe in these pages.

Tried and convicted on bogus charges that included conspiracy to commit espionage and, in the case of Gerardo Hernández, conspiracy to commit murder, the Five spent sixteen-plus years helping to lead—by their own conduct and example within prison walls—the international "jury of millions" that came together in the fight to win their freedom.

On December 17, 2014, that battle ended in victory. The US government commuted the sentences of Gerardo, Ramón, and Antonio, the three who remained behind bars on US soil. They were welcomed home in a spontaneous explosion of joy as millions of Cubans poured into the streets. "From that moment on," Antonio said, "all the time in prison was erased."

The year since their release has been one of sharing the joy of being reunited with their loved ones—a victory, in René's words, "against the extreme cruelty of the most powerful empire in history," which attempted to "separate, destroy, divide, and humiliate our families." It has also been a year of "coming down to earth," as Ramón has said, learning firsthand from the people of Cuba and the world as they "land and get up to speed," leaving the years of walls and bars behind.

For Cuba, the release of the Five was a precondition for responding to a shift in Washington's fifty-five year policy of refusing to recognize the legitimacy of the government and institutions established by Cuba's victorious socialist revolution. On the day the Five were reunited on Cuban soil, Cuban president Raúl Castro and US president Barack Obama announced that diplomatic relations between the two countries, broken by Washington in 1961, would be reestablished.

In making that announcement, Obama acknowledged that the political course implemented by eleven administrations, both Democratic and Republican, had failed to achieve the US rulers' objectives. Despite decades of US-orchestrated economic strangulation, attempted diplomatic isolation, political slander, and provocations—not to mention years of terrorist operations, assassination attempts, a failed invasion, and even the threat of nuclear annihilation—Cuba's toilers still refused to submit to Washington's dictates. It was time to try different methods.

■

It's the poor who face the savagery of the US "justice" system: The Cuban Five talk about their lives within the US working class is not an account looking back on the hardships of prison or the battle that won their freedom. It looks to the future, addressing something even more important.

What is it that enabled the Cuban Five to act as they did over those sixteen years? What prepared them to set the example they did?

Suddenly, in September 1998, they were not only Cuban revolutionaries, living and working in the US precariously and temporarily like other immigrant workers, at the same time that they carried out important work in defense of their homeland. In a single day, they became Cuban revolutionaries and communists deeply immersed in the US working class.

Like millions of others, they experienced firsthand the meaning of capitalist "justice" in the US—what Ramón calls "an enormous machine for grinding people up." In the United States, which has the highest incarceration rate in the world, right now, today, some seven million men and women—a number equaling nearly two-thirds of Cuba's population— are either living behind bars or shackled to some kind of court-supervised probation or parole.

"We lived in a microcosm of the outside world," Gerardo notes. "We came to know problems of many places."

Over these years, the Five learned about the class struggle in the United States from the inside. And this included the discovery, to their own surprise as Ramón writes, of the impact of the victorious Cuban Revolution—from its very first years—on important layers of workers and youth in the United States.

It's the poor who face the savagery of the US "justice" system addresses the realities of class relations in the US without exaggeration or distortion, as the Five draw on their own experiences with an uncommon depth of understanding, objectivity, and humor.

■

"Anyone can write a poem," Antonio tells students at the main science and engineering university in Havana. "But to spend seventeen months in the hole and sixteen years in prison and create paintings that don't contain a shred of hatred . . . that's a product of the way we were educated as revolutionaries. It's something we were able to achieve thanks to the revolution."

Antonio's words express one of the most important things readers will find here. As Antonio and René tell the students, nothing equipped them for that morning in September 1998 except the Cuban Revolution itself and the course followed by the revolution's leadership from its outset. What prepared them was the education and values (the proletarian internationalist education and values, I would say) that they had internalized as young people growing up in Cuba.

"Let's take, for example, the situation in which we found ourselves when we were arrested in 1998," Antonio says.

> They put some guy in front of you asking you to admit to something you didn't do. He tells you that if you "cooperate," you can get back all the material things you had, you'll go back to your normal life.
>
> If not, the man tells you, "We're going to give you such a long sentence that you're going to die in prison."
>
> So you have to be prepared for this. You have to have already developed within yourself an understanding of what you will do at such a moment. Once you pass that test and say no, you begin to realize you're happier than those around you. People see you and say, "Damn! Why are you laughing all the time? Why are you so happy?"

The prisons of the ruling classes are not unknown territory for working people fighting to defend their interests. That fact is amply confirmed by the frame-ups and mass incarcerations that have marked strike battles, insurrections, national liberation struggles, and proletarian revolutions around the world for a century and more. How revolutionists, communists, conduct themselves in prison, however, is always a test anew. Towering figures like South African revolutionary leader Nelson Mandela and Cuban leader Fidel Castro are both examples, as is Malcolm X coming from a different trajectory.

The account that follows opens a window on the political lives of the Five behind bars. The example they give us is worthy of study and emulation.

There is no romanticism of prison life in these pages, no pretense US penal institutions are anything but unreformable instruments of class retribution and punishment. There is no pretense they are anything but a grotesquely magnified reproduction of the social relations, values, and "business practices" of the dog-eat-dog capitalist world that have spawned the US "justice" system. And that includes the controlled fostering of violence, gangs, drug trade, and racism to "organize" prison life and break the spirit of the human beings incarcerated.

The vast prison network spread across the US is but the forerunner of the horrors imposed on other people's lands in places whose names have become infamous, such as Guantánamo, Abu Ghraib, Bagram.

One of the most powerful sections of the book is the stories of fellow Cubans the Five met in prison in the US, not a few of whom had spent time behind bars in Cuba as well. "In US prisons they aim to dehumanize you; in Cuba a prisoner is another human being," sums up the diametrically opposite social relations and class values they describe.

Within US prison walls, the Five also enjoyed solidarity and respect, won through the acts of respect and solidarity they extended to others. Their account is peppered with examples. Many readers will be surprised to learn, as René notes, that "all of us were able to do our time without any problems from officers or other prisoners." But that was not preordained. It's an expression of the social norms they internalized and acted on as Cuban revolutionists.

In Cuba, "it's normal for people to help each other, to cooperate with each other," Ramón says. "It's not a question of a 'good policy.' It's simply a fact," the consequence of a revolution that overturned the cutthroat social order of capitalism, and of a leadership that for decades has maintained that course against all odds.

That is the example Gerardo, Ramón, Antonio, Fernando, and René brought with them into their lives within the US working class.

∎

Unlike revolutionaries imprisoned for political acts in many countries, the Five did not enjoy the luxury of serving their time together. As the cover painting by Antonio depicts, they were sent to "five distant prisons." After receiving their draconian sentences—three of them life without parole—Gerardo and René never saw any of their brothers again. Antonio, Ramón, and Fernando spent only a brief time together at the Miami federal detention center in 2009 when they were brought in for resentencing hearings.

The fact that each of them was on his own for so many years—and yet they acted as one—provides an additional gauge of the strength of their political habits and moral stature.

"I promised myself that I'd use the time in prison for my own benefit," Fernando explains, "that I'd leave with my mental and physical health intact. . . . I spent a lot of time reading. . . . I told myself over and over that just because I was passing through prison, I didn't have to become a 'prisoner.'"

"The jailers want to destroy you. They want to break your physical, moral, and mental integrity," René notes. "You learn the first day that you have to resist this, and that the measure of your victory in doing so will be to leave prison a better person than when you walked in. Each of us, according to our own individual characteristics, adopted that as our strategy."

And that is exactly what they accomplished. They didn't become "prisoners." They didn't turn in on themselves. They turned outward with pride and confidence. They broke through the prison bars, sustaining their freedom through reading and study, art and poetry, writing and drawing, running and handball, chess and parcheesi. They corresponded with their tens of thousands of supporters across Cuba and reaching to every corner of the world.

And above all they reached out with respect, with solidarity, and with their own example to fellow workers in prison, to the human beings with whom they shared their daily lives and struggles for the better part of their adult years.

Today, René tells students in Havana, that history "is now in the past. We are five Cubans like any of you. We will take our place in the trenches and, like each of you, we will be judged by the work we do."

Whatever that future brings, the Five have not only written a new page in the history of the Cuban Revolution. They have added an immensely important page to the history of the US working class as well, another intertwining of the class struggles in our two countries.

For that we thank them and the Cuban people they exemplify. In every sense, their example will bear fruit.

January 7, 2016

None of the Five sought
applause, rewards, or fame

Havana, February 24, 2015. President Raúl Castro decorates Gerardo Hernández, Ramón Labañino, Antonio Guerrero, Fernando González, and René González "Heroes of the Republic of Cuba."

"The honor we receive today is at the same time a summons demanding that we meet the new challenges the revolution faces." *—Gerardo Hernández*

Five soldiers, loyal to the ideas of Martí, Che, Fidel, and Raúl

GERARDO HERNÁNDEZ

At a February 24, 2015, ceremony in Havana, President Raúl Castro presented Gerardo Hernández, Ramón Labañino, Antonio Guerrero, Fernando González, and René González each with the medals "Hero of the Republic of Cuba."

The National Assembly of People's Power, Cuba's legislature, had awarded the Cuban Five that distinction more than thirteen years earlier—on December 29, 2001, just days after a US federal court had sentenced each of them to draconian prison terms, including life imprisonment for Hernández, Labañino, and Guerrero. Presentation of the medals, however, had to await the victorious outcome of the worldwide campaign to free them. They were decorated at a ceremony in Havana marking the hundred twentieth anniversary of the beginning of Cuba's third war for independence from Spain, in 1895.

Below is the text of Gerardo Hernández's remarks on behalf of the Five, addressing more than 2,000 fellow Cubans and international guests and a live television audience of millions.

■

Dear compañero Army General Raúl Castro Ruz, President of the Councils of State and Ministers; compañeras and compañeros:

Honoring the Cuban men and women who, exactly one hundred twenty years ago, decided to take up arms once again to fight for the homeland's independence is the best way to accept the honor "Hero of the Republic," which has generously been awarded to five Cubans of these times whose merit was simply to have fulfilled our duty.

José Martí, the soul of that national uprising of February 24, 1895, said the measure of a hero is the respect paid all those who have been heroes. Thus, our first thought today is one of gratitude and loyalty to those throughout history who, with their sacrifice, have made it possible for us to live in a socialist, revolutionary, victorious Cuba, conscious that it is up to our generation and those to come to defend the continuity of this revolution, which embodies the dreams and ideals of our liberators.

The first thoughts of the Five today must be for a man whose leadership and strategic vision were decisive to the battle that led to our freedom, and whose example instilled in us a spirit of struggle, resistance, and sacrifice. A man who taught us that the word surrender does not exist in the dictionary of a revolutionary, and who, very early on, assured all Cubans that the Five would return to the homeland. Commander-in-chief: This distinction, which we proudly receive today, is also yours.

To our Army General Raúl Castro, who did not rest until what Fidel had promised was accomplished, and to all the men and women who, like him, already wear this honorable star on their chests and were always an example to the Five, we say: This distinction is also yours.

To the Cuban people who made the cause of the Five their own, and who today continue to encourage us with their support and affection; to the leadership of our country's party and government; to the mass organizations, institutions, attorneys, religious bodies, figures and governments of other countries that stood in solidarity with our cause: This distinction is also yours.

We also thank our sisters and brothers throughout the world who fought shoulder to shoulder with us over sixteen years of legal and political battles. We say: This distinction is also yours.

To our families, who struggled, suffered, and firmly resisted for so many years, and to all those who deserved to see this day but are no longer among us: This distinction is also yours.

To the faceless heroes and heroines who will never be able to receive a public tribute such as this, but who have dedicated, dedicate, or will dedicate tomorrow their lives to the defense of the country from their anonymous trenches: Be assured, wherever you may be, that this distinction is also yours.

This honor we receive today is at the same time a summons demanding that we rise to the occasion to meet the new challenges the revolution faces. More than a few times since our return, compatriots have approached us to say they would have liked to have had the opportunity the Five had to protect our people from aggression. To them, and to all Cuban patriots, we say our mission has not ended—all can join in.

The updating of our economic model in an effort to achieve a more efficient, prosperous, and sustainable socialism, as well as the process of reestablishing relations with the United States, create a moment of change demanding all of us to act with intelligence, professionalism, commitment, and conviction, to identify and confront the new challenges and new perils that are coming.

There are and will be many ways to defend Cuba, and Cuba will always need loyal sons and daughters to protect her. It is encouraging to us to know that in the heart of this revolutionary people there are many "Five" willing to sacrifice everything for their homeland.

With Ramón, René, Fernando, and Antonio, together we accept with pride and gratitude this great honor the homeland confers upon us. The homeland can count on these five soldiers who today, before our people, reaffirm our commitment to serve you until our last days, and to always be loyal to the ideas of Martí, of Che, of Fidel, and of Raúl.

They received their distinctions because they didn't seek them

FIDEL CASTRO

Cuban leader Fidel Castro released the following remarks to the press March 1, 2015, after meeting in his home with Gerardo Hernández, Ramón Labañino, Antonio Guerrero, Fernando González, and René González.

■

I received them on Saturday, February 28, seventy-three days after they set foot on Cuban soil. Three of them had spent sixteen long years, taken from the prime of their youth, in the damp, foul-smelling, and repulsive depths of US prisons after being sentenced by venal judges. The other two, who likewise had tried to forestall the empire's criminal attacks against their homeland, were also sentenced to many years of brutal imprisonment.

US investigative bodies, devoid of the most basic sense of justice, took part in the inhuman persecution of them.

Cuba's intelligence services had absolutely no need to track the movements of a single piece of US military equipment. At the Lourdes Radio Electronic Monitoring Center, located south of the Cuban capital, they could observe from space everything moving on our planet. This center can detect any moving object thousands of miles from our country.

February 28, 2015. Cuban leader Fidel Castro greets the Five at his home. Counterclockwise from right, Fidel Castro, Gerardo Hernández, Ramón Labañino, Alejandro Castro, Fernando González, René González, Antonio Guerrero.

"The Five antiterrorist heroes never did any harm to the United States. They worked to anticipate and prevent terrorist acts against our people organized by the US intelligence agencies the world knows so well." —*Fidel Castro*

The Five antiterrorist heroes never did any harm to the United States. They worked to anticipate and prevent terrorist acts against our people organized by the US intelligence agencies the world knows so well.

In carrying out their work, none of the Five Heroes sought applause, rewards, or fame. They received their distinctions because they didn't seek them. They, their wives, parents, children, brothers and sisters, and fellow citizens—we all have a legitimate right to feel proud.

In July 1953, when we attacked the Moncada barracks [of the Batista dictatorship], I was twenty-six years old and had far less experience than they have shown. If they were in the US, it was not to harm that country or to take revenge for the crimes being organized there and the explosives being stockpiled to use against our country. Attempting to prevent these attacks was absolutely legitimate.

The main thing they did upon arrival was to greet their families, friends, and the people, without putting aside for a moment a rigorous medical checkup and paying attention to their health.

I was happy for hours yesterday. From the group headed by Gerardo and aided by them all, I listened to amazing tales of heroism, including from the painter and poet, whom I had met while he was working on one of his construction projects at the airfield in Santiago de Cuba. And their wives? Their sons and daughters? Sisters and mothers? Wasn't I also going to receive them? Well then, their return and joy must also be celebrated with their families.

Yesterday, before anything else, I wanted to talk with the Five Heroes. For five hours that's what we did. Since yesterday I've fortunately had time to ask them to invest part of their immense prestige in something that will be extremely useful for our people.

It's the poor who face
the savagery of the
US 'justice' system

Havana, August 17, 2015. Antonio Guerrero, Gerardo Hernández, Ramón Labañino, and Fernando González discuss their experiences within the US working class with Mary-Alice Waters, Pathfinder Press (center); Rafaela Valerino, Cuban Institute for Friendship with the Peoples (far right); and Róger Calero, Pathfinder (photographer). Interview continued with the Five, including René González, in December.

"In the United States the judge will often give you the stiffest sentence allowed just because you went to trial, just for not pleading guilty. Everything we're talking about here is the product of capitalism.... There's no solution within the US justice system, no reform that will change it."

—Antonio Guerrero

PART 1

The reason there are
so many in prisons in the US
is not the amount of crime

MARY-ALICE WATERS: December 17, 2014, marked a hard-won victory for the Cuban people and supporters of the Cuban Revolution all over the world. That was the day that three of you—Gerardo, Ramón, and Antonio—were welcomed home by millions of Cubans who poured into the streets to celebrate. And the day Cuban president Raúl Castro and US president Barack Obama simultaneously announced that diplomatic relations between the two countries, severed by Washington in January 1961, would be restored.

In the months since then, all five of you have been traveling throughout the island thanking the Cuban people for their solidarity and their years of defiant resistance, without which your freedom could not have been won. You've also been drawing on your own experiences in the United States to explain what the word "capitalism" means—in human terms.

Each of you worked and lived for a good part of your adult life in the United States. Before you were framed up and imprisoned, like many other immigrant workers you had jobs in construction, as janitors, as deliverymen, in restaurants and hotels, or doing whatever work you could find "off the books."

Later, during your long years in prison, you were part of

Havana, May 14, 2004. Contingent of high school students from Camilo Cienfuegos Military Academy joins massive march repudiating US government sanctions aimed at strangling the Cuban Revolution. Sign reproducing photo of humiliating torture of Iraqi prisoner by US soldier at Abu Ghraib prison, near Baghdad, says, "In Cuba, this will never happen."

that very large section of the US working class that is either currently behind bars or has served time at some point in their lives. Today that's over six million people—5 percent of adult males, and nearly 17 percent of adult men who are African American.

Around the world, many people have seen photos of the degrading, inhuman treatment meted out to inmates at Abu Ghraib in Iraq and the US prison camp at Guantánamo. What they often don't understand is that these institutions of imperialist brutality mirror prisons inside the US whose names are infamous among US working people—places like Attica, Clinton, Beaumont, Florence, Angola, and Pelican Bay. US foreign policy begins at home.

When you speak about life in the US, you speak with authority, and not only here in Cuba. Your words ring true to millions of US families as well. They've lived similar experiences.

Antonio's paintings, depicting scenes from your seventeen months in isolation cells in Miami and your nearly seven-month trial, are a good example. They strike a deep chord.

These are things we want to talk about, starting with the capitalist "justice" system you came to know so well.

In one of René's first interviews when he was able to return home to Cuba in 2013, he explained that in the United States just going to trial, rather than agreeing under pressure to plead guilty to some charge "negotiated" by the prosecutor and your attorney, earns you a lot of respect in prison. Was that the same experience all of you had?

FERNANDO GONZÁLEZ: When someone is arrested in the US, a high percentage are "overcharged." They're accused of many more things than they might have done. It's a tool consciously used by prosecutors. People find themselves in a situation where some charges—for crimes they probably never committed—will be dropped if they plead guilty to other charges, which they also may never have committed.

Prosecutors pile up charges against you. The law not only allows that; it's how the entire system is organized. It's a tool to force you to plea bargain.

Most of those arrested in the US end up with court-appointed lawyers, since they can't afford an attorney. The lawyer usually advises you to plead guilty, even if it might be better for you to go to trial.

Why? Well, one reason is that if you plead guilty, then all the court-appointed attorney has to do to get paid is to go to court three or four times, at most. He has to be there at the indictment, the plea agreement, and the sentencing. But if you go to trial, the lawyer will probably end up spending at least three weeks in court.

The whole system—even the lawyer who's supposed to be looking after your interests—pressures you to plead guilty.

There's another side to this. Let's say you're already in the federal court system, as we were. You're there in court, and they bring in a witness. He says he has spent fifteen years in the Drug Enforcement Agency or the FBI or whatever. He comes in wearing a suit and tie, not a hair out of place, and sits there with an air of "nice guy." He swears he'll tell the truth—and then tells one lie after another. Who is the jury going to believe? They'll believe the cop, of course, not the defendant.

In many cases the defendant has already been the victim of a barrage of unfavorable news coverage. Anxieties about crime here, there, and everywhere are bolstered by the press.

GERARDO HERNÁNDEZ: We saw many cases like that. We met many people who said, "Look, I was no angel. I was doing 'this' and 'this.' But I never did 'that' or 'that,' much less the murder I'm serving life for."

"But when I told that to the attorney appointed by the judge," the person would continue, "the lawyer said: 'No jury is going to believe you. Take the offer they're making and do the time. That's the best you can do. If you don't, they'll slap you with the maximum sentence.'"

"They say that straight up."

My last cellmate was a guy from Mexico. From the beginning the court-appointed lawyer told him to plead guilty—to murder no less. He asked, "How can I plead guilty to kidnapping and murder if I didn't do it?"

He's now serving two life sentences for something he didn't do. He showed me his court papers. There was a letter from the mother of the man who was killed. She asked the prosecutors not to try those people, because she knew they weren't the ones who killed her son. But the defense lawyer never presented the letter to the court.

One piece of the prosecutor's evidence was a jeep the young Mexican was said to have been given in payment for the murder. He has papers showing the jeep belonged to his cousin's wife; she'd owned it for years. But the lawyer didn't introduce those documents at the trial. That gives you an idea of what kind of representation he had.

Most lawyers stick with a program that says, "Don't go to court because you'll lose." If the client is courageous enough to say, "No, I'm innocent. I'm going to trial," they'll try to convince him it's suicidal.

RENÉ GONZÁLEZ: Not every lawyer is like that, of course.

RÓGER CALERO: All of you had court-appointed lawyers, didn't you?

RENÉ GONZÁLEZ: Yes, and they did a good job. It's interesting what happened with these lawyers. At first they came to us and said, "Look, take a plea bargain. Others are already agreeing to testify. They're going to incriminate you in things you didn't do."

But each of the five of us said "no." So little by little, Phil Horowitz, who was my lawyer, and the others realized we really were determined to go to trial. When they saw the evidence, they also realized it was a farce—none of us had committed espionage. None of us had killed anyone or conspired to kill anyone. So they defended us during the entire trial and then on through the rounds of appeals.

ANTONIO GUERRERO: Many of the prisoners are Latinos and don't know English; others are basically illiterate. That cranks up the pressure to cop a plea, since you can't read the documents in any language.

I remember when we were in the Federal Detention Center in Miami, three Russian men were arrested. And a young woman, too. They'd been selling caviar. They had a license and everything, including documentation for the caviar they'd imported and sold. The guy I talked with had no idea what hit him—suddenly he found himself in prison.

The one who seemed to be the head of the group wanted to go to trial. They were innocent, he said. But that's not how it works, I told him. If you go to trial, they'll bring in some witness against you. It doesn't have to be from the FBI. It can be someone who wants to cut a deal with the prosecutors—get a few years off his own sentence. They'll put him on the witness stand, and he'll swear you did this or that.

What's more, the judge more often than not will give you the stiffest sentence allowed, just because you went to trial. It's an additional punishment for not pleading guilty. Everything we're talking about here, and we're talking specifically about the United States, is the product of capitalism.

There are prisons in every country. But the reason there

The lawyers fought for us like lions

I wasn't happy with my first court-appointed attorney. He seemed ambivalent. I told him, "Look, I need to know if you're prepared to defend me courageously, because I need someone who'll work to get out the truth. We're going to denounce the terrorists; we're going to denounce the people who control Miami." Little by little he withdrew from the case.

Later I was represented by William Norris. I met him during our seventeen months in the hole, and from the first moment he made a good impression on me. . . . I promised I would tell him everything I could about our mission and that I'd never lie to him. . . .

In truth, he and the other attorneys fought for us like lions.

RAMÓN LABAÑINO
ESCAMBRAY NEWSPAPER
NOVEMBER 13, 2015

Leonard Weinglass always insisted that ours was essentially a political case, and he warned us from the start that the fight would be long and hard. His experience with the "system" had taught him that. For our part, even beyond the professional relationship we always thought of him as a compañero in the battle for justice.

GERARDO HERNÁNDEZ,
VICTORVILLE, CALIFORNIA
MARCH 23, 2011

When I accepted this case I had no idea what I was getting into, what René was getting into, and what the fam-

(Continued on next page)

ilies were getting into. People have asked me, have you ever had a case like this before? I never have. I never will again. Cases like this come once in a lifetime.

PHILIP HOROWITZ
LONDON
MARCH 8, 2014

Attorneys for the Cuban Five included *Martin Garbus* and *Paul McKenna* (for Gerardo Hernández); *Jack Blumenfeld* and *Leonard Weinglass* (for Antonio Guerrero); *William Norris* (for Ramón Labañino); *Richard Klugh* and *Joaquín Mendez* (for Fernando González); and *Philip Horowitz* (for René González).

are so many prisoners in the United States is not the amount of crime. It all begins with the arrest, indictment, and plea bargain. That's where people begin to be chewed up. There's no solution within the US justice system, no reform that will change it. It's not a system that metes out justice to those who've committed a crime. Every day you see the detention center in Miami fill up due to the circumstances many people face. Unfortunately, this system provides a livelihood for many.

RAMÓN LABAÑINO: To understand the American system of justice, you have to begin from the fact that it's a system used by the US government to enable a powerful minority to control a vast majority who are poor and dispossessed.

Almost 40 percent of the state and federal prison population in the US is African American, and more than 20 percent is Latino. In some states and some prisons the percentages are even higher. The whites in prison are poor, too. You may come across a rich person, a politician, here and there, people doing minimal time for white-collar crimes—and with all the protection in the world. A person who is poor—Black, Latino, Native American, white—faces the enormous savagery of what's called American justice.

It serves above all to sustain a system that has no solution for the poor, present or future. It's a way to separate them from society. It's a way to hold off a revolution, to keep the conditions for a genuine revolutionary struggle from emerging.

In the United States, imprisonment is a way of dehumanizing a human being. It's a way of isolating you from society, including from your family. To make you feel alone. To make you feel depressed. To make you feel as if you have no one to turn to. To make it easier to obtain a guilty plea.

An individual ends up isolated from everything, not knowing how to confront this monster.

You're not innocent until proven guilty. It's the opposite. You're guilty unless, with great difficulty, you can prove you're innocent.

You're up against a system. Think about the name they give the indictment—for example, *United States of America v. Gerardo Hernández et al.* The US government, with all its machinery and resources, comes down on you like a ton of bricks. They give you a jury selected in ways that favor the government. And in the end they're going to convict you, since you're considered guilty from the outset.

From the beginning there are all sorts of ties between the defense attorney, the prosecutor, and the judge. The first thing a defense attorney does when he gets a case is to go talk to the prosecutor and ask, "What do you want to do with this guy?"

Supposedly the government always tells the truth, right? The reality is that it's an enormous machine for grinding people up. Faced with it, the great majority of people—95 percent, if you take state and federal prisoners together—plead guilty. Five percent or fewer go to trial, and of those the big majority lose.

MARY-ALICE WATERS: According to the most recent figures, 93 percent of federal trials end in convictions. Figures for local and state courts are somewhat lower, and vary greatly from one area to another, but the average rate of conviction is around 85 percent.

> *The American system of justice serves above all to sustain a system that has no solution for the poor. It's a way to prevent conditions for a revolution emerging.*

GERARDO HERNÁNDEZ: I'd like to add something on plea agreements. Someone who hasn't had the experience of being in prison and doesn't know how the system works might find it hard to believe that a person who hasn't committed a crime is going to stand in front of a judge and say, "Yes, I did it."

It's not unusual for legal cases in the United States to involve more than one person. There are often codefendants. The prosecutors use the principle of divide and rule. From the very first day they begin to pressure everyone separately. More often than not they manage to break one of the defendants, perhaps the weakest, most nervous, most vulnerable person. "Look," they tell him, "we know you didn't do it, but it's better to say 'yes' because it is better to serve ten years than forty. With a forty-year sentence you'll never get out of prison. Or worse, you might even get a death sentence."

When they get one person to "confess," they go to the others and tell them, "Look, your codefendant says yes, you all did it. He'll testify to that. Who do you think they are going to believe?"

So the man thinks, "Well, I didn't do it, but how can I stand up in court and say that my friend"—sometimes it's a brother or cousin—"is testifying that we did it because he's scared? I better plead guilty, too. Otherwise they'll throw the maximum sentence at me."

ANTONIO GUERRERO: Of those few who go to trial in the federal courts, there's another thing involved. Some of them would like to strike a deal with the prosecution, whether they have done something or not. But they can't because it puts their family at risk.

Say they've charged a number of people with being involved in a drug ring. One of them goes to trial and then another and another. The rest of the defendants can't plead guilty because the prosecutors will try to force them to implicate others. And the consequences of pleading guilty, even if you pretend you're not going to implicate others, can cause problems for your family on the outside.

RENÉ GONZÁLEZ: Keeping us in the "hole" for seventeen months in Miami after we were arrested gave the prosecution a big advantage in court. They used a perverse scheme of putting us in one hole at the detention center, and keeping the evidence in another little room across the street that we began calling the "second hole." We were allowed only a few sessions with our attorneys to review all that material, discuss the charges against us, and prepare the details for our trial.

Above all they used the hole, as they do with everyone they throw behind bars, to try to make you feel helpless, to make you wonder whether you're going to be able to survive in prison. In our case there was the added factor that we repre-

US capitalist 'justice' ... some facts

World's jailer-in-chief

• World's highest incarceration rate: US has 4.4% of world population but 22% of world's prisoners.

• Some 7 million people (1 of 35 adults) are today in federal or state prisons or local jails (2.2 million), or on parole or probation (4.8 million).

• 5 percent of adult males and 17 percent of adult males who are Black are or have been behind bars.

'Plea bargains' and the right to a trial

• 97% of federal and 94% of state convictions in criminal cases result from the accused pleading guilty to charges horse traded by prosecutors and defendants' lawyers.

• In federal cases in 2003, defendants insisting on their right to a trial got sentences averaging nearly three times longer than those taking a "plea bargain" (12.5 years vs. 4.5 years).

Life sentences, death row, and the 'hole'

• More than 10 percent of US prisoners are serving life sentences, nearly a third life without parole.

• Some 1 in 20 state and federal inmates are in the "hole," solitary confinement, or other punishment cells (2005).

• 2,984 people are on death row (2015).

Class, race, and incarceration

• The vast majority of those behind bars are from the working class. Some 40% are Black.

• 1 in 10 men in their 30s who are Black is in jail or prison any given day.

sented Cuba. The visceral hatred they have for us for being Cubans and communists made them try their best to break us in those long initial months, to get us to "confess." They failed.

Going to trial gives you some standing among other prisoners. They say, "This man stood up to the government." And that's a big help. They know it means you won't finger them. Wardens and guards encourage snitching among the prisoners, including among those who are serving life sentences. They encourage prisoners to blame others, or to assist the government's prosecution. They call that "taking Route 35"—shorthand for what's euphemistically referred to as a "Post Sentencing Cooperation Agreement."

Treatment in the Miami prison was really abusive, cruel. I don't like to use the word torture—I'm not light-minded about the language I use—but cruel it was. Cruel and unusual punishment. That's the term used for treatment prohibited by the Eighth Amendment to the US Constitution. They did it to create leverage in the trial. They tried to break us, to make us give in to their blackmail, their pressure. But we came out stronger than when we went in. We had firmer moral principles than they did.

After the Miami trial, in general we were treated like any other prisoner. We weren't subjected to cruel treatment simply because of who we were. Except that in March 2003 they did put each of us back in the hole for a month, in even worse conditions than in Miami, because the federal government called prison authorities and told them to put us in punishment cells. Coincidentally, they did this when we were preparing our appeals to the circuit court in Atlanta, with an April 7 deadline. So that action also prevented us from communicating with our lawyers.

MARY-ALICE WATERS: Gerardo, March 2003 was the month

They offered us everything if we would betray Cuba

Gerardo Hernández

We spent the first seventeen months in punishment cells, what prisoners call the "hole." In my opinion, they never planned to keep us in prison for so long. They always believed we would betray the Cuban Revolution. . . .

Just imagine what would have happened if they could have gotten five Cuban intelligence officers, or however many they could break, to sit in front of a TV camera and read a script—to say Cuba has chemical weapons, or Cuba was planning a terrorist action against the US. Any outrageous lie they could think up.

These were dangerous years when Cuba was practically isolated. It would have had quite a serious negative impact.

That was their aim. They offered us everything if we would betray Cuba. But when the five of us held firm, they sent us to the punishment cells.

EUROPEAN PARLIAMENT TV STUDIO
BRUSSELS, BELGIUM
SEPTEMBER 16, 2015

Washington launched the Gulf War, the second US war against the Iraqi regime of Saddam Hussein. The invasion was launched on March 19, to be exact. Beginning February 28 you and the others were sent to the hole by order of US attorney general John Ashcroft, on the grounds that your contact with other people "could pose a threat to the national security of the United States." Later "press leaks" from US intelligence sources accused Cuba of "stealing US secrets on the preparations for the invasion of Iraq and passing them to Saddam Hussein's government." And Washington expelled fourteen Cuban diplomats.

What did they tell you about the reason you were being sent to the hole?

GERARDO HERNÁNDEZ: I was still at Lompoc in California at the time, working in an office in the factory that made signs. Lompoc was an old institution, in very poor condition.

Prison officials gave me no reason. I recall that a lieutenant came looking for me at the factory there. As he was walking me to the punishment cell, the officer asked, "Why are you going to the hole?"

"You're asking me?" I said to him.

The order came from "on high," but I never knew from where. The aim was to keep us under the Special Administrative Measures they use for those charged with terrorism—SAM procedures, as they're called.

They told me to sign some papers listing all the rules, which included, among other things, total isolation. At first they put me in a regular cell in the hole, but then they saw that the prisoner who cleaned there, a Cuban, passed me a book, flip-flops, and a little instant coffee under the door. So they took me from there and sent me to a basement *below* the hole, a place others in the prison called the "box."

It was a section of ten cells with double doors—one with bars, the other solid metal. They held the worst cases there, including prisoners who'd lost their minds, were chained to beds, and were occasionally injected with sedatives. There was no way to know if it was day or night. I was held with the lights on twenty-four hours a day, with only my underwear as clothes, and with nothing to read. When somebody flushed the toilet in the cell above me, filthy water dripped down the walls of my cell.

The papers prison officers had given me to sign said I'd be held there for a year. The case would then be reviewed, they said, and those conditions might be extended another year. Three days later, however, they moved me out of the "box," again with no explanation.

International solidarity played a very important role. There were so many protests that even several US congressional representatives contacted the prisons where each of us was being held and asked for information about what was happening. We were held under those conditions until the end of March.

MARY-ALICE WATERS: What about the time you were put in the hole at Victorville?

GERARDO HERNÁNDEZ: That was in 2010, in late July—again, without any explanation. Nobody would tell me anything. Finally, after much questioning by my attorneys and others, the authorities said the prison had received a letter addressed to me from Cuba containing a white powder, and that I was in the hole pending an investigation.

Victorville, as you may know, is in the California desert, and in the middle of summer the temperature outside sometimes hit 110 degrees Fahrenheit. They put me in a cell with air conditioning so defective that my cellmate slept on the floor just to breathe the air coming in under the door. And that wasn't true just in my cell, but a group of them.

Attorney Leonard Weinglass was able to visit me at Victorville at the time. And when the conditions under which I was being held became known in Cuba, protests began to be organized there. Fidel went on TV to condemn what was happening to us. Calls started coming in to prison officials from CNN, BBC, and other big news outlets, as well as from US congressional offices. Compañeras and compañeros in the United States and other countries also raised their voices in protest.

All of you were my oxygen

August 3, 2010

Dear Sisters and Brothers:

I am dictating these words via telephone, which is why I must be brief and I will not be able to say everything I would have liked.

Yesterday afternoon I was removed from "the hole" with the same speed with which I was thrown in. I had been taken there supposedly because I was under investigation. These investigations can take up to three months, sometimes more, but I was there thirteen days. As a well-known Cuban journalist would say: you can draw your own conclusions . . .

I want to express to all of you my deep gratitude. You know that they were particularly difficult days due to the excessive heat and the lack of air, but all of you were my oxygen. I can't find a better way to summarize the enormous importance of your solidarity efforts. . . .

GERARDO HERNÁNDEZ
US PENITENTIARY
VICTORVILLE, CALIFORNIA

While the stay in the hole for an "investigation" is usually three months, they released me August 2. The next day I was able to get on the telephone and dictate a message thanking all those in Cuba and around the world who had demanded that I be released from isolation.

RÓGER CALERO: René, you experienced one aspect of the US "justice" system that none of your brothers did. You served your entire fifteen-year sentence—thirteen years and twenty-four days with time off for good behavior, which by law they had to give you. Then, in addition, you were ordered to serve three years of court "supervised release" and ended up having to spend a year and a half more in the United States before the court ruled you could return to Cuba if you renounced your US citizenship.

RENÉ GONZÁLEZ: In my case, the "supervised release" amounted to another attempt to isolate me as a human being. Every parolee confronts restrictions on who you can associate with, where you can live and travel, and other harsh conditions. But these were particularly onerous because of the circumstances I faced.

First of all, you're supposed to tell anyone you meet that you're an ex-convict. Doing so, of course, would have made it easier for anyone who opposed our struggle to find me. So I couldn't talk with neighbors, since I'd have to tell them, "I'm René González. I just got out of prison." That would have started the ball rolling… "And why were you in prison?"

I couldn't even get a driver's license or a credit card, since I'd have to give my name and address.

I was forced to shut myself up in a house that someone, out of solidarity, allowed me to share. It was a comfortable house but a golden cage nonetheless. It was a really difficult situation.

"Solidarity was mutual. We offered support in prison and we received it too."
—Gerardo Hernández

CINCO DE MAYO

Cinco De Mayo program 2012
12:00 pm-2:30 pm

Hosted By T. Weeks, Recreation Specialist

E. Marmolejo, Recreation Specialist

Schedule of Events

Opening Ceremonies : Jesus Arreola & Theogan Garner
Tribute in song to Richie Valens Performed by T. Weeks
Cinc De Mayo Speaker : Armando Quiroz
Musical Performance by : "Ilusions"
History of Cuba an Mexico : Gerardo Hernandez
Musical "Rap" Azteca De Oro : Alberto Chaia
Who is Pancho Villa ? : George Johnson
Musical Performance by "Dead To Rights"

PHOTOS COURTESY OF GERARDO HERNÁNDEZ

"It took an effort, but prisoners from various countries and religions got authorization to commemorate holidays. I was often invited and on several occasions asked to speak." *—Gerardo Hernández*

Top: Hernández speaks on historical ties between Cuba and Mexico at "Cinco de Mayo" event, Victorville penitentiary, May 2012. **Left:** Program for the event. **Bottom:** Hernández (right) receives certificate of participation from Recreation Specialist Tony Weeks. The paintings of Muhammad Ali and Martin Luther King (by an artist in the prison) were used at events to commemorate "Black Heritage."

"We earned the respect of others, including Cubans and even prison officers, because we treated others with respect."
—René González

"African Americans at the prison would say to me, 'I read in the *Militant* you were in Angola. That Cuba was there to support the liberation of African people. You have our full support. If you have any problem, just let us know. If you need a table to sit at in the cafeteria, you can sit with us.' We encountered many instances like this."
—Gerardo Hernández

Top: Hernández (center) at Victorville, 2006, with African American prison mates Brasco, Burks, Red, and Pope. **Bottom:** René González (left) with Cuban Rodolfo "Roddy" Rodríguez (kneeling in Cuban 5 T-shirt he made), and another friend at Marianna prison in Florida. "René never tried to impose his thinking on me or anyone else," said Rodríguez. "But if you asked his opinion he would tell you."

COURTESY RAMÓN LABAÑINO

COURTESY RAMÓN LABAÑINO

COURTESY GERARDO HERNÁNDEZ

"One question many people ask us is, 'How did you get along with other Cuban prisoners?' because they know there were many who had left Cuba. They simply can't imagine what this would be like."
—*Gerardo Hernández*

Top: Ramón Labañino (center) with other Cubans at Jesup, Georgia, July 2012. **Middle:** Labañino with a Cuban friend who is Muslim at Ashland, Kentucky, January 2014. **Bottom:** Hernández and two prison mates in Lompoc, California, June 2003. "Both came in the Mariel boatlift," wrote Hernández. " 'I may or may not like the system in Cuba,' some would say, 'but I respect what you did.' "

> "We lived in a microcosm of the outside world. We got to know problems that, unfortunately, are common to many countries."
>
> —*Gerardo Hernández*

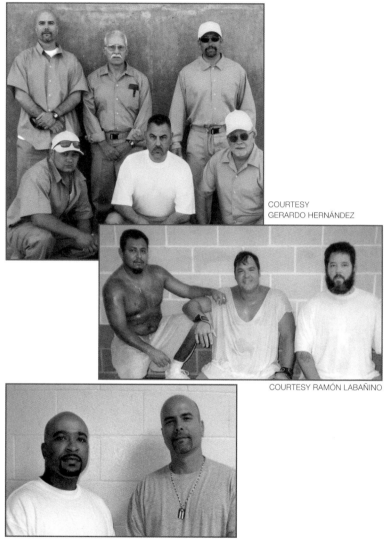

COURTESY
GERARDO HERNÁNDEZ

COURTESY RAMÓN LABAÑINO

COURTESY GERARDO HERNÁNDEZ

Top: Hernández (standing, left), with prison mates in Victorville. **Middle:** Labañino (center), after playing handball with Mexican and Cuban friends, Beaumont, Texas, August 2008. **Bottom:** Hernández with "Papa" in Victorville, February 2012. "His daughter was writing a school paper about Cuba and asked him to have a picture taken with me," Hernández wrote.

PART 2

In US prisons they aim to dehumanize you; in Cuba a prisoner is another human being

RÓGER CALERO: In the federal prison system, inmates are required to work, right?

RAMÓN LABAÑINO: That's correct. You have to have a job of some kind. I did all sorts of things. I started out as an orderly, doing cleanup jobs. I taught Spanish to English speakers. I was a janitor in the laundry room. I worked for a while cleaning and straightening up the recreation area.

The better-paid jobs are with UNICOR. That's the trade name for Federal Prison Industries, a government-owned corporation going all the way back to the 1930s. More than half of federal prisons have factories run by UNICOR. Inmates are paid from $0.23 to $1.15 an hour.

It's a terrific deal for the government. A cheap workforce locked up in prison, with no right to organize, no health or safety protections. Nothing.

Inmates in these factories make uniforms, clothing, shoes, office furniture, even military items—and are paid a fraction of the federal minimum wage, which is $7.25 an hour right now. What a gold mine! It's all part of the US justice system.

MARY-ALICE WATERS: And a window onto the workings of capitalism! You had experience with that kind of class exploitation before your arrests too. René worked jobs in construction and on road repair crews. Antonio worked in a

49

"UNICOR is a terrific deal for the government. A cheap workforce locked up in prison, with no right to organize, no health or safety protections."
                                                                    —*Ramón Labañino*

Gerardo Hernández in front of Federal Prison Industries (UNICOR) factory in Lompoc, California, November 2003. More than 100 of these government-owned factories are located in federal prisons. Pay is between $0.23 and $1.15 an hour.

restaurant kitchen, then at a Days Inn, later digging ditches, and finally—through a temp agency—as a janitor at the Boca Chica Naval Air Station in Key West. We've read about that last job, since prosecutors used it as "evidence" in their espionage conspiracy frame-up.

RAMÓN LABAÑINO: In Tampa, when I first arrived in the US in 1992, I delivered newspapers door-to-door and sold shoes for a mail-order business. When I was assigned to move to Miami in 1996, I ended up driving a van delivering medicine and other merchandise to pharmacies. That was the most steady job I had.

I should also clarify one thing. In their eagerness to go after Gerardo, the prosecution turned him into the head of the entire network. That's how they portrayed him. Actually he was the head of one group, and I headed another. They concocted a giant insidious case against Gerardo. They wanted a scapegoat for the incident with the planes.*

GERARDO HERNÁNDEZ: In Miami, my cover was that I was a freelance graphic designer. To maintain that appearance, I often left home early and well dressed and then returned in the afternoon.

But I never really worked. Given the assignment I was carrying out, and the number of agents I was responsible for, it would have been difficult to hold a job. Not only could I end up getting an urgent coded beeper message at any time, but

---

* On February 24, 1996, the Cuban air force shot down two small planes over the country's territory that had taken off from southern Florida. Those flights were the latest of a growing number of violations of Cuban airspace organized by Brothers to the Rescue, a Miami-based group of Cuban counterrevolutionaries. After multiple warnings to Washington by the Cuban government to halt these provocations, Cuba's air force fired on the planes after the pilots refused repeated orders to turn back.

it was dangerous for me to show up on the radar screen of the Internal Revenue Service. I didn't have a story that would hold up under the kind of scrutiny they carried out.

A couple of times I did some work for a Brazilian newspaper in Miami, but my pay was "off the books." I did that so I could produce some illustrations from a few newspapers, if need be, to help keep up my cover.

RÓGER CALERO: What about the jobs you and others had in prison. How many hours a day did you work?

RAMÓN LABAÑINO: You normally work from eight to five. But often there's overtime. During the war against Iraq, for example, there were a lot of orders for clothing and boots. The factory at the Beaumont penitentiary in Texas worked practically around the clock.

FERNANDO GONZÁLEZ: At the federal prison in Oxford, Wisconsin, where I spent five and a half years, the factory assembled electronic components and systems for rockets, fighter jets, and tanks.

ANTONIO GUERRERO: You have to have a job, but sometimes it's hard to find work and you have to wait for someone to leave. In prison you never take a job somebody else already has. And we never took the jobs that paid a little better, since they were a source of income for other inmates—and a source of conflict for that very reason. Like jobs in the kitchen, where people stole things.

In the penitentiary at Florence, Colorado, where I spent eight and a half years, they needed someone to give classes in math and in English as a second language, so I did that. Later, I worked as a teacher at Marianna, because some inmates asked me for help in passing the tests given in Spanish to get their GED [General Educational Development] certificates, the equivalent of a high school diploma. I wasn't working for the prison then. I did it for those individuals, who together paid me $15 a month. More Latino students got their GEDs with the help of the course I taught than during practically the entire history of Marianna.

MARY-ALICE WATERS: US prisons are organized to exact retribution. To punish. They try to destroy a person's dignity and sense of worth.

FERNANDO GONZÁLEZ: That's exactly right.

GERARDO HERNÁNDEZ: The road to rehabilitation does not exist in the US prison system.

RAMÓN LABAÑINO: What happens when you enter the prison system? The first thing they do is to isolate you—from society, from your family.

In the US prison system, the road to rehabilitation does not exist.

I'd say most people in federal prison lose contact with their families within a few months. Most families don't have the economic resources to support someone in prison. There are families that overcome these obstacles, of course, but many others can't.

With no family support, no money beyond the pittance you make in prison, you become more and more isolated. You become "institutionalized," as they say. You made a mistake in life, or at least that's what they convicted you of, but now you've got no choice but to take on the rhythm of the prison. The prison becomes your world.

On top of that, inside prison you're threatened by gangs—like poor kids are who grow up in most US cities. They extort money from you, for one thing. "Listen," someone tells you, "if you're going to survive here, you've got to pay me $10 a month." Under those pressures you can become an animal—a prison animal. Some join the gangs just to get along, or in other cases they prefer to join a church. That's another way to try to cope in that environment.

Some start selling drugs because it's a way to make money in prison. Others become card sharks, gamblers. The system forces them in that direction by taking everything from them.

If you want to appeal your conviction or your sentence, you have to look for someone to help you with the paperwork. And you have to pay for that too. A motion costs $200 dollars. That's an ordinary motion. If it's complicated, you pay $500. Where are you going to get that kind of money? You join a gang, start extorting people yourself. That's how a human being becomes an imprisoned being, inside as well as outside.

RÓGER CALERO: You pay that to the lawyer representing you?

FERNANDO GONZÁLEZ: No, usually to a fellow prisoner, a jailhouse lawyer.

RAMÓN LABAÑINO: They're prisoners just like you, but they have experience preparing motions. And let me tell you, some are very good at it. I knew of prisoners who have gotten people released.

FERNANDO GONZÁLEZ: In fact, Mumia has a very good book titled *Jailhouse Lawyers.** But there are also a lot of swindlers.

RAMÓN LABAÑINO: Yes, exactly. In a maximum-security prison—where the average sentence is eighty years, ninety years, or life—you're surrounded by people who have a brutal mentality. It's a fight for survival. If you have the will to

---

* Mumia Abu-Jamal was framed for the 1981 killing of a Philadelphia police officer and spent thirty years on death row before being resentenced to life in prison without parole.

improve yourself, you can do it. But it has to come from deep inside you.

MARY-ALICE WATERS: There's no better example of that than Malcolm X.

RAMÓN LABAÑINO: Yes, for sure.

RÓGER CALERO: What about the drug trafficking?

RAMÓN LABAÑINO: While I was in prison, I saw a documentary about prison wardens. One of them said openly that he knew there were drugs in the prisons. The authorities know some prisoners are addicts, who need the drugs to live. Some are both addicts and dealers. The wardens allow a certain amount of drugs through in order to keep things calm. They know how the drugs come in, who brings them in. When the level gets too high, they shut things down.

RÓGER CALERO: The drug trafficking is part of the same capitalist system. It's a business. Prison authorities use it for their own purposes, and often profit from it.

FERNANDO GONZÁLEZ: It's the same with the gangs. The prison administration uses them, as in US society in general. In a city like Chicago, for example, it's better for the government if rival gangs are fighting among themselves in Black neighborhoods, and with gangs in Latino communities too. Much better than if Blacks, Latinos, and whites all got together and started to think about who the real enemy is.

MARY-ALICE WATERS: We've had some experiences here in Cuba that are the opposite of what you've been describing. We have a friend in Matanzas, for example, a university professor who also gives classes in prison and takes pride in it. She told us about using some books Pathfinder has published in her classes and the interest they generate. We've read about Silvio Rodríguez and other musicians giving concerts inside the prisons.

In Santiago de Cuba, after hurricane Sandy in 2012, when

we were walking through one of the neighborhoods speaking with people, we met a group of construction workers sitting in the shade, eating lunch. We stopped to talk, and they told us, "We're prisoners. We're working here on day release, building housing for families that lost their homes."

We know things in Cuba are far from perfect. But social relations—the way people relate to each other—are the opposite of what you experienced in the US. And that's true in the prison system too. In Cuba the revolution carried out by the workers and farmers eliminated the economic and social system built on class exploitation, on retribution and punishment, social isolation, punitive deprivation of medical care, denial of culture and education. That's why the US government is so determined to punish the Cuban people and destroy your example.

GERARDO HERNÁNDEZ: We were with many Cuban prisoners in the United States who had been inmates in Cuba as well. Some had come to the US as part of the Mariel boatlift in 1980.[*] Others were *balseros*—"rafters"—who crossed the Florida Straits on perilous contraptions of all kinds during the economic crisis of the 1990s. There were about twenty Cubans at the Lompoc federal prison in California when I was sent there in 2002. Six of them were in my unit. They'd often

---

[*] Some 128,000 Cubans came to the US in April 1980 during what was known as the Mariel boatlift. As part of its escalating drive to reverse the 1979 revolutionary victories in Nicaragua and Grenada and snuff out intensifying class battles elsewhere in the Americas, the US government cranked up a propaganda campaign alleging that Havana was blocking Cubans from leaving the island. The revolutionary government called Washington's bluff, opening the port of Mariel to private boats coming from the US to pick up anyone who wanted to emigrate. The exodus included Cubans who had served time for nonviolent offenses. US rulers demanded that Havana stem the outflow.

say, "Yes, material conditions in prison"—especially in the
newer ones—"are a lot better than where I was in Cuba."

Obviously you can't compare living conditions in the rich-
est country in the world with the economic resources in Cuba.
But most of them recognized that prison personnel here in
Cuba make a real effort to rehabilitate inmates, to help them.
In the United States, a prison counselor is someone who puts
in his hours at work and does his best not to ever have to see
you.

"In Cuba," they'd point out, "when my family came to visit,
my counselor (here we call them re-educators) would ask for
permission to sit with us. He'd talk with my wife and ask how
the little girl was doing in school, what problems there were
at home. He'd tell her how I was doing in prison."

That doesn't happen in the United States. The counselor is
there to fill out forms for you and spends the day trying to
make sure you don't come to him with a problem. When you
do, he glares at you with a sour face.

The human part is essential. I often give the example of a
young neighbor of mine. When he was in high school, he was
involved in something that rarely happens in Cuba—what's
known in the US as "bullying." He was studying in the coun-
tryside on a scholarship program and he was being pestered
and harassed. One day he took a knife, scuffled with the other
boy, and stabbed him in the wrong place, killing him.

That boy was sentenced to seven years. During that time he
completed high school and went on to university. Every day
they took him by bus from the prison to the university cam-
pus. He took classes all day, and the bus brought him back to
prison. Today he is free and working as a psychologist.

I used the example of this boy with my prison mates.
"Cuba," they'd say to me, "when I was in prison back home I
was able to go visit my family on a pass. If a relative died, they

gave you a pass. Sometimes I'd spend the weekend at home. Other times I'd work on the outside."

I recently had a conversation with a very prestigious young artist here in Cuba, Mabel Poblet. She showed me some samples of her work. One stood out to me—an installation with hundreds of red plastic flowers. "Look at these flowers," she said. "They were made by a woman who is a prisoner in Holguín."

"We visited the women's prison there and met an inmate, Betsy Torres, who was making flowers," Mabel said. "I had in mind doing an installation using flowers, so I asked her to make some for me—the ones you see here. After she was let out for good behavior, I invited her to the opening of my exhibition."

This type of exchange is the opposite of the dehumanization that takes place in the US prison system. People are given the opportunity to reintegrate and rehabilitate themselves. What you see more often in the United States is that people who come in for a petty crime are made into real criminals inside the prison.

FERNANDO GONZÁLEZ: I'll give you another example of what inmates in the US who'd previously been in prison here in Cuba would tell us. They'd say that if your family came to see you in a Cuban prison, and there was a fellow prisoner whose relatives haven't been able to visit, you can invite him to join you and your family and share the food they brought. In the United States that's not allowed.

Look at what the Bureau of Prisons calls its Program Statement. It says the Bureau of Prisons encourages social contact with the outside. But in practice it's the opposite. They put up obstacles to everything, including visits.

It's not enough that the prisoner is 1,500 miles or more from his family. It's not enough that many families can't afford a plane ticket and a weekend in a motel to come see you.

On top of all that, the searches and other alienating procedures family members and friends have to go through to get into the prison, not to mention the tense, uncomfortable layout of the visiting room—everything conspires against any notion that social contact with the world outside is "encouraged." They seem to do everything possible to *discourage* anyone from coming to see the prisoner.

ANTONIO GUERRERO: We shouldn't be one-sided. Prisoners sometimes spoil things, too. Some aren't concerned about the consequences their actions can have for others. I'll give you an example of something that happened one day at the prison in Florence.

In the penitentiary, during the era of DVDs, of CDs, they installed five or six tables with CD players. A little room where you could take your headphones and ask for a CD to listen to. Of course, getting a cubicle was a big hassle. They were in great demand. In this case, it turned out that the little motor in the CD player could be used to make a tattoo gun. One day, when there was a distraction someone loosened two small screws, opened the player, and took out the motor. It no longer worked, of course.

GERARDO HERNÁNDEZ: "The most important difference, what I miss most," some Cuban inmates in the US would tell us, "is that in Cuba I had the right to conjugal visits, or to get a pass to see my family." But not in the United States.

In federal prisons and in all but four of the fifty states, something so elementary as conjugal visits are not permitted. If they were, it would greatly reduce tensions. It would humanize people. It would be an incentive for good behavior.

RAMÓN LABAÑINO: Under the capitalist system in the United States, the way they educate a prison officer is very different from how a prison officer is educated in a socialist society like

Cuba's. In the US, the officer is there to take care of himself
and to make sure the prisoner doesn't escape. The prisoner is
supposed to suffer—that's why he was sent there.

They don't care whether there's money in the budget for
another handball court. That's a big issue I had, since—in addition to reading, studying, and playing chess—sports was
one of the ways I handled all those years in prison. I exer-
cised, lifted weights, and played lots of handball. But prison
officials didn't want to paint the floor of the handball court
with the kind of rubber compound that makes it easier on
your knees.

That's how I injured my knee, in fact. But medical care in
prison in the US is terrible; they don't want to spend money
on that either. I went to the doctor and he told me, "Take two
aspirin. Put ice on it, keep your feet up, and tomorrow you'll
be better." They only really take care of you when you're on
the verge of dying. (Today my knee is much better, by the
way, more agile. I don't have pain. To celebrate July 26, I even
climbed Turquino Peak, the highest mountain on the island
here.*)

There's money in the budget to buy better food for the cafeteria too, but it's never fully used. I know. I worked in the
cafeteria several times.

Actually, I didn't like working in the cafeteria, because a lot
of people take those jobs in order to steal food. But we don't
steal. It's not our philosophy, not the social values we learned
in Cuba. With what I ate I had enough. Frankly, I'm no good
at stealing.

---

* Climbing Turquino Peak, in the Sierra Maestra mountains of
eastern Cuba, has long been an expression of revolutionary commitment. The mountain is topped by a monument to José Marti,
Cuba's national hero.

Here in Cuba it's different. Our officers may not have resources, but they are trained to really help you. I'd venture
to say that ethic goes far beyond the framework of the prison
system to the broader society here.

In Cuba a prisoner is another human being. He's someone
who made a mistake and is in prison for that reason. It's not
like the US, where the prison population is the enemy—just
as uniformed officers there see the people as the enemy. Why?
Because on some level they understand there could be a social revolution in the United States some day. And their job is
to contain that revolution, in order to protect the social layer
that's in power.

That's pretty elementary. You don't even need Marxism-
Leninism to see that. But if you don't understand this, you'll
never see why things happen the way they do in the United
States. Why the police act the way they did in Ferguson, Missouri, last year. Why there's no solution within that system.

The police may seem like part of the common people, but
because they have a uniform and get paid a little more, they
feel like they're part of the better-off layers of society. They're
trained to see the people as the enemy. Their first thought
when they see somebody Black is, "He's going to kill me."

In Cuba those things don't happen. Why? Because it's normal for people to help each other, to cooperate with each
other. It's not a question of a "good policy." It's simply a fact.
It's why we accomplish a great deal with very few resources.
In the United States you can provide all the resources in the
world to the prisons and it wouldn't change anything. There
won't be conjugal visits or other humane conditions. Why?
Because one man is there to punish the other.

FERNANDO GONZÁLEZ: In Miami we saw women who were
pregnant when they were arrested. When the time came to
give birth, they were taken to the hospital . . .

RAMÓN LABAÑINO: . . . in chains.

FERNANDO GONZÁLEZ: Yes, *in chains*. They gave birth in the hospital, and two days later they were brought back to their cells without their baby.

> *You can provide all the resources in the world to US prisons and nothing would change. There wouldn't be humane conditions. Why? Because one man is there to punish the other.*

Recently I visited a women's prison here in Cuba, at Guantánamo. Before the visit, some compañeros who work there asked me for any advice I had. I told them I couldn't give them any, because the ethics of the revolution made our conditions the opposite of what I'd experienced in prisons in the United States.

When they took me to the women's prison, I was really surprised. In the United States, you know from miles away you're near a prison. You see the walls, fences, razor wire, towers, lights, surveillance vehicles. But in Guantánamo, as we got closer, I asked, "Where's the prison?" There was a wall you could easily jump over. Even as fat as I am, I could have jumped over it!

Inside, some rooms are like small apartments. If a woman is pregnant—or becomes pregnant, because they have conjugal visits—she can stay in one of those rooms until the baby is a year old. It's a small room with a kitchen, where she can cook. The prison provides food for the baby and other necessities. There's also a sewing shop.

GERARDO HERNÁNDEZ: After the first year, the child is taken to live with other members of the family, if possible. If not, then until the mother is released, those children live in a home for kids who have no families to look after them. While we were in prison in the US, we received letters from some children in Cuba who at first I thought were orphans, but actually were living in one of these homes.

I remember a young girl named Anita, whose mother was in prison. The director of the home later wrote us that Anita would no longer be there. She was leaving the following month, since her mother had completed her sentence and was being released.

In Cuba the state pays for the care of the child in a home like that, and takes care of their education, until the mother finishes her sentence.

Message from Ramón Labañino to Troy Davis family and supporters

Brothers and sisters,

We feel deeply the horrific execution of Troy Davis.[*] It is another terrible injustice and stain on the history of this country. We join in the pain felt by his relatives, friends, and brothers across the world. Now we have another cause, another flag, to pursue our struggle for a better world for all, free of the death penalty and barbarism.

In Troy's honor, and in honor of all the innocents of the world, we must continue, united, until the final victory!

Our most heart-felt condolences.

Five fraternal embraces,

On behalf of
ANTONIO GUERRERO
FERNANDO GONZÁLEZ
GERARDO HERNÁNDEZ
RENÉ GONZÁLEZ
RAMÓN LABAÑINO
SEPTEMBER 23, 2011

SAVANNAH MORNING NEWS

Troy Davis, at 1991 trial.

[*] Troy Davis was executed September 21, 2011, on frame-up charges of killing a policeman in Savannah, Georgia. No physical evidence linked him to the killing. Seven of nine non-police witnesses against him later changed their testimony; several said police pressured them to falsely finger Davis. An international campaign fought the execution, and Davis won several stays of execution. But courts rejected a new trial and President Obama refused to intervene. Davis maintained his innocence to the end.

PART 3

We extended solidarity to others in prison and we received it too

RÓGER CALERO: What's the maximum prison sentence that can be imposed in Cuba?

GERARDO HERNÁNDEZ: The longest sentence is now life. It used to be thirty years, but a life sentence was added to the Penal Code in 1999.

FERNANDO GONZÁLEZ: Only a few very serious crimes have life in prison as the sentence. No more than a handful of people are serving life terms right now. Capital punishment has not been taken off the books, but it has been used very rarely in Cuba over the past thirty years—and not at all since 2003.

MARY-ALICE WATERS: In the United States the length of prison sentences has increased enormously the last thirty years. The number serving life sentences has gone up by 80 percent, and for nearly a third of them—like the sentence given to Gerardo, and to Antonio and Ramón until overturned on appeal—it's life without parole. Ramón's statement that the majority of inmates at Beaumont were serving sentences in the range of eighty to ninety years is mind boggling.

To that you have to add the increased use of solitary confinement. At one notorious state prison in California, Pelican Bay, as of 2012 more than half of the 1,000-plus inmates had been in solitary confinement for five years or more, and 8 percent for between twenty and forty-two years! In California as a whole, nearly twelve thousand prisoners—some 7 percent of the total—are in isolation. It's all part of the system based on retribution and punishment.

As for the death penalty in the United States, it's still used as a weapon of terror against working people. More than nine hundred people have been executed since you were arrested in 1998—last year alone there were thirty-five, and another seventy-three death sentences were handed down. Some three thousand prisoners are on death row in state and federal prisons.

GERARDO HERNÁNDEZ: Also, there are at least 2,500 minors in the United States serving life sentences without the possibility of parole. They may be more than eighteen years old now, but not when they were given life sentences. And they were sentenced in adult court.

MARY-ALICE WATERS: Hundreds of thousands of workers in the United States have children, brothers, nephews, fathers, or other relatives who are confined to prisons they'll never leave. All of us have relatives, friends, comrades, neighbors, or co-workers whose families live with this.

RAMÓN LABAÑINO: I want to say something about the psychological impact on a human being of being told you're going to serve a life sentence. It's designed to dehumanize you. You're going to die there in prison, they tell you. There's no way out.

Suicides among those who've just been handed long sentences aren't unusual. Someone hanged himself when we were in the Miami Dade detention center. I remember it perfectly.

FERNANDO GONZÁLEZ: They put his body in front of our cell.

RAMÓN LABAÑINO: Yes, he was a young Black man. He'd been sentenced to twenty-five years, a prison term he could

The Cuban Revolution is inspired by a spirit of justice not vengeance

Raúl Castro

President of the Council of State and Council of Ministers
First Secretary of the Communist Party of Cuba

This morning, at the proposal of the Political Bureau, the Council of State decided to commute the death sentences for a group of convicts. They will serve life sentences instead, except those who committed their crimes before the sentence of life in prison became part of our [1999] Penal Code, who will serve thirty years instead. Some convicts have been waiting several years for a decision by the Council of State.

This situation is mainly the result of the policy in force since the year 2000 of not applying the death penalty, a policy that was interrupted only in April 2003 to put a complete stop to the wave of more than 30 attempts and plots to hijack airplanes and vessels, encouraged by the policies of the United States, which had just begun its war on Iraq. . . .

This decision has been adopted not on account of pressure but as a sovereign act, in harmony with the humanitarian and ethical conduct that has characterized the Cuban Revolution from the start, inspired always by a spirit of justice and not vengeance, and knowing, moreover, that comrade Fidel is in favor of the abolition of the death penalty for any type of crime, when the appropriate conditions exist, and is opposed to the extrajudicial methods that certain well-known countries use without shame.

(Continued on next page)

This does not mean that we are removing capital punishment from the Penal Code. On different occasions, we have talked about this issue, and the opinion has always prevailed that under the current circumstances, we cannot disarm ourselves in face of an empire that is constantly targeting and attacking us.

Terrorism against Cuba has enjoyed total impunity in the United Sates. It is truly state terrorism.

APRIL 28, 2008
SIXTH PLENUM OF CENTRAL COMMITTEE
CUBAN COMMUNIST PARTY

We're moving toward a future when the death penalty in Cuba will be abolished

Fidel Castro

Here, no one is ever, ever punished out of revenge. Among our punishments we also have life sentences, which is an alternative to capital punishment. . . .

I think we're moving toward a future in our country when we'll be able to abolish the death penalty. So one day we will be among those countries that have eliminated it. We aspire to that not only on philosophical grounds, but out of a sense of justice and reality.

MY LIFE
INTERVIEW WITH FIDEL CASTRO
BY IGNACIO RAMONET
(SIMON AND SCHUSTER, 2006)

have completed physically. But some people can't deal with a long sentence like that. It's one of the sources of violence, of murders and rape.

In Beaumont, for example, two or three young prisoners got together and raped a female guard. They jumped her and hit her with some locks. She was one of the best officers in the prison. A decent, quiet person.

These were young people—twenty, twenty-two, twenty-five years old—who would never be out on the street again. They had life sentences and would never again have sexual relations outside prison walls. That's something that really dehumanizes you.

FERNANDO GONZÁLEZ: It's related to what we talked about earlier—plea bargaining. Congress passes laws setting mandatory sentences. So what's your option, then? You don't want to risk serving that enormous amount of time, so you plead guilty. You cooperate with the government. And they reduce your sentence. It's that way by design, not by chance.

RÓGER CALERO: In 2012, one of the US Supreme Court judges issued an opinion in which he confirmed just what you're raising—that plea bargaining has become "not an adjunct to the criminal system; it *is* the justice system" in the United States. Long sentences are designed to win convictions.

MARY-ALICE WATERS: Yet in the midst of all this, there's also solidarity among prisoners. Your own experiences provide many examples. We know from interviews you've given, as well as tributes to you by others at the prisons where you served, that you helped people there and they helped you. You helped Cubans reconnect with their families, for instance. You won the respect of many.

I'm reminded of the way the press in the US covered the horrendous conditions in New Orleans in the wake of Hurricane Katrina in 2005. Almost all they wrote about was the

---

Plea bargaining is not part of the US justice system: it *is* the system

Supreme Court Justice Anthony Kennedy

"Ninety-seven percent of federal convictions and ninety-four percent of state convictions are the result of guilty pleas. The reality is that plea bargains have become so central to the administration of the criminal justice system that defense counsel have responsibilities in the plea bargain process. . . .

"To a large extent . . . horse trading [between prosecutor and defense counsel] determines who goes to jail and for how long. That is what plea bargaining is. It is not some adjunct to the criminal justice system; it *is* the criminal justice system."

OPINION OF THE COURT
MISSOURI v. FRYE
MARCH 21, 2012

---

violence and fear, how terrible things were. They rarely even whispered about the countless acts of kindness and solidarity thousands of working people extended each other, as they sought together to restore life and dignity.

It would be useful to talk about how you functioned in the midst of the challenges faced in prison.

GERARDO HERNÁNDEZ: Solidarity was mutual. We gave support and we received it, too. Reconnecting families, for example. You mentioned that.

One example that comes to my mind was a man named Ángel. Angelito, as we called him, was relatively young. He left Cuba on the Mariel boatlift in 1980 and had spent several years in prison in the United States. The veins on his arms had scars, and one day I asked him about them. He told me he'd tried to kill himself four or five times and had been taken to the hospital, bleeding.

When he was seven or eight, Angelito had been brought from Cuba to the United States by his mother and stepfather. Before that he'd been raised by his grandmother in Cuba, and left two sisters behind here. When he got to the US, his step-father became jealous and wouldn't let his mother call Cuba. She and Ángel lost all ties to their family.

When Ángel's mother died, his stepfather abandoned him. He began to commit crimes and landed in prison. He was completely alone. I asked him for the name of his family and where in Havana he had lived. He told me the name of a movie theater close to where he'd grown up.

So I spoke with my mother-in-law, who lives near that area. She found the house where the family had lived, but they had moved. She kept looking and eventually sent me some information.

"Angelito," I said, "I've got bad news and good news. Which do you want first?"

"The bad news," he said.

"One of your sisters died. Your grandmother, too."

He began to cry.

"The good news is that your other sister is here in the United States," I said. "She's been looking for you for years. Here's her phone number."

Still in tears, Angelito asked me to go with him to the chap-lain's office to see if they'd let him make a phone call—he had no money to pay for the call himself. We went and the chap-lain dialed the number on the spot. Angelito got in touch with his sister.

His behavior started to change completely. Before he'd frequently received disciplinary write-ups. When Angelito asked to transfer to the state where his sister lived, authorities told him they'd move him if he kept a clean slate for six months. He did. The last I heard, he was in the same state as his sister and she had visited him.

RENÉ GONZÁLEZ: We were on good terms with the big majority of inmates who were African Americans. In prison, relationships are usually based on mutual interests. No one gives you something for nothing. A prisoner asked me to review a legal document, for instance. We went over it together, and I translated it for him. When he tried to pay me, I said no. He was shocked. That one incident became known to others and affected their attitude toward me.

I remember an African American who ironed clothes for other prisoners to earn a few dollars. With me, he refused to accept payment. It was a way of saying, I respect you. You've been consistent, you haven't been broken, you always help others.

We never had any problems, that's the fact. Our prison mates knew we wouldn't snitch on them, so they trusted us. If there was going to be trouble, someone would warn you. "Don't go near such and such place," they'd say. Or they'd tell you, "Look, put aside some water. Something's going to happen between two gangs, and there will be a lockdown." All of us were able to do our time without any problems from officers or other prisoners.

GERARDO HERNÁNDEZ: We didn't walk around the prison telling people about our case, of course. But thanks to the *Militant*, to books published by Pathfinder, and other publications that made their way into the prison, people learned about our fight. Eventually the case of the Five became known in every federal prison. Either someone had been in prison with one of us, or had been in prison with someone who had been—or they had read about us.

"Hey, Cuba," someone would tell me, "a new guy came in from such and such prison and knew Ramón—or knew Fernando, knew Tony, knew René—and wants to meet you." Or someone who'd read about the case and wanted to meet me. We had many experiences like that.

African American inmates would come up to me and say, "I read an interview in the *Militant* that says you were in Angola. That Cuba was in Africa to support the liberation of the African people. Were you part of that?"

"Yes, I was," I'd tell them.

"I want you to know you have our full support. If you have any problem here, just let us know. If you need a table to sit at in the cafeteria, you can sit with us. If you need a cell, you can live with one of us. There's no problem."

We encountered many, many instances like this in all the prisons we were in.

I remember one experience in particular. There was a prisoner with one of those SS tattoos in Lompoc, where I was held the first few years after the trial. One day he saw me reading the *Militant* and we started talking; I gave him the paper.

"I'm going to subscribe," he said.

I told him, "When you read what's in the *Militant* [*laughing*], you'll ask for your money back!"

We left it at that. He ended up being sent to the hole, and they sent me to Victorville. We didn't see each other after that. Then, last year, in 2014, almost ten years later, he came to Victorville. And he was a subscriber to the *Militant*!

"Hey," he said, "I've kept up with everything that's happened to you."

I didn't believe it at first. But one day he told me, "I just got the paper, and there's an interview with you, an article about your case." He used to get his subscription before I did, since prison officials held up my mail and sent it through the Special Investigative Services [the federal prison police force].

RAMÓN LABAÑINO: Solidarity began when other prisoners found out who we are. Let me give an example.

After we were given those enormously long sentences in December 2001, we knew the prisons we'd be sent to were going to be rough places. That was especially true for Gerardo, Antonio, and me, since we had life sentences.

We were concerned we might be confronted by people who were anticommunist, anti-Fidel. I was sent to the penitentiary at Beaumont, Texas—known as "Bloody Beaumont," I was told.

When I arrived, the warden began interrogating me.

"So, you're a political prisoner," he said. "You hate President Bush." He was trying to provoke me. I started laughing.

"So you think you're a tough guy?" The warden said he was sending me to the hole for a week, and when I got out, he was going to put me in the unit "with the worst Cuban here, the guy who runs the prison."

The warden did in fact send me to the hole for a week. I made friends there with two African Americans who told me the rules of the unit, its codes and dangers.

When I got out, I was already dreading this Cuban—who I thought for sure would be a counterrevolutionary who'd make trouble for me. I arrived at the unit and saw a skinny guy sitting there, with an open shirt. You knew he was Cuban as soon as you saw him—cocky, slouching, self-assured. It was something I'll never forget—that image of him, with a bodyguard there on each side of him.

"Hey, you. Come over here!" He said it with an attitude.

"I'm going to have to fight him," I thought. I put my bags down and walked over to him. When I was five or six feet away, he said, "Are you one of those five spies of Fidel's?"

"Yes," I said, calmly. "I'm one of Fidel's five men. Is there a

COURTESY GERARDO HERNÁNDEZ

COURTESY RAMÓN LABAÑINO

"The case of the Five became known in every federal prison thanks to the *Militant*, books published by Pathfinder, and other publications that made their way in. Either someone had been in prison with one of us, or had been in prison with someone who had been—or had read about us." —*Gerardo Hernández*

Eladio Bouza ("Fantomas"), a Cuban, with Hernández at Lompoc, California, 2003 (left), and with Labañino at Beaumont, Texas, January 2008 (right).

"With the Jesup squad," says Ramón Labañino, July 2011—all the Cubans at that Georgia federal prison. Clockwise from top left, Diosdado, Santy, Labañino, Miguel, Shorty, and Lázaro.

"In a number of cases we helped Cuban prisoners get in touch with families they'd lost contact with. It was a mutual relationship.... I keep in touch with friends I made in prison."
—Ramón Labañino

problem with that? If so, let's settle it right now. What do you want to do about it?"

I thought there was going to be a fight. Instead, he jumped up and said, "My brother! You guys are tough!"

The important thing was what he said next: "Because you're Fidel's men."

He knew that meant we were determined and loyal. He knew we'd stood firm through a nearly seven-month trial. We didn't cop a plea. We stood up to the system. We weren't going to turn and run.

The guy's name is Alejandro Maíz—I don't think there's a problem saying that publicly. He did twenty years and was released. From that first moment, Maíz helped me with everything. He taught me how things ran, what to do if a situation came up. He still writes me from Miami. He asked me for photos. He wants to give them to his parents.

We were also respected for being communists. Just like Gerardo described, one of the African American inmates soon came to me and said, "Hey, let us know if you need anything. Let us know if you run into problems."

And the Muslims, too. When Louis Farrakhan, the Nation of Islam leader, visited Cuba, some inmates from the Nation came to see me. "We're with you," they said. "Let us know whatever you need. No one will bother you here."

We never went looking for trouble, of course. And little by little we won increasing support, to the point of physical protection.

As Gera said, in a number of cases we helped Cuban prisoners get in touch with families they'd lost contact with. They were grateful. It was a mutual relationship. I keep in touch with friends I made in prison. One called me yesterday, in fact.

At some point they may have committed a crime. But they're the kind of people who when Cuba, or Fidel, or the revolution comes up, they defend their country. If the US ever invades Cuba, one of them told me, "we're gonna rise up."

We found solidarity like that wherever they sent us.

RENÉ GONZÁLEZ: Prison was a learning process for all of us. We set a goal to leave prison stronger than when we entered.

> *Prison was a learning process*
> *for all of us.*
> *We set a goal to leave prison*
> *stronger than when we entered.*

The jailers want to destroy you. They want to break your physical, moral, and mental integrity. You understand that immediately. You learn the first day that you have to resist this, and that the measure of your victory in doing so will be to leave prison a better person than when you walked in. Each of us, according to our own individual characteristics, adopted that as our strategy.

RAMÓN LABAÑINO: You have to draw on your inner reserves. If you sink into the negativity of prison—if you feel sorry for yourself—it will destroy you.

RENÉ GONZÁLEZ: For me, the hardest thing at first was making sure I didn't react the way they wanted me to. It didn't take long. The turning point came when my daughter turned fifteen. I'd saved up my weekly minutes to make sure I had enough to call her that day. We were in the hole, however, and they figured out a way to deny me the call.

That night I suffered, but when I woke up the next day I was a different person. I realized I couldn't allow myself to suffer because of their actions. And when I finally was able to call,

I told my wife that from then on, if I could communicate, that would be fine, but if I couldn't, that would be fine, too.

I realized that if I thought that way, I'd be in control, not them. I'd remind myself that I had very strong moral values, and that they could never change that. Like Ramón, I also turned to physical exercise—I ran a lot—and to reading to load up my intellectual backpack.

GERARDO HERNÁNDEZ: One question many people ask us is, "How did you get along with the other Cuban prisoners?" They ask because they know we were in prison with Cubans who had left the country—and some people simply can't imagine what that would be like.

A prisoner might say, "Look, I left Cuba because I didn't like communism. I didn't want to have anything to do with it." There were a number of people like that.

Others would say, "I left Cuba on the spur of the moment, and now I'm sorry I did. I'd go back if I could."

Others said, "I wanted to see the world." Or "I went to look for a better life."

But there was a common denominator. "I respect what you did," almost all of them would say. "I may or may not like the system in Cuba, but I have family there. When someone sets off a bomb, they don't care whether it blows up a communist or someone who isn't a communist. I don't want anything to happen to my mother, or my grandmother. So I respect what you did."

ANTONIO GUERRERO: From the moment we were convicted, people in Cuba began to hear about our case. The billboards began to go up. People learned about the seventeen months in the hole and the seven-month trial, which we faced with tranquility and dignity.

We began receiving hundreds of letters, not only from Cuba but from the US and around the world. There was news about us in various publications. All that started getting known in the prisons, too. And apart from that, other prisoners could see we were ordinary human beings, that we didn't create problems for anybody. To the contrary, we were the easiest people in the world to get along with. We helped others. And, of course, we had our own opinions.

RENÉ GONZÁLEZ: Most important, I think, was our conduct. We earned the respect of others, even Cubans and prison officers, because we treated others with respect. If that's how you act, and if you keep away from certain activities—like drinking, using drugs, gambling—people respond by showing respect in return.

ANTONIO GUERRERO: One of the things I did was play chess. There were people who played for money. The best chess players bet on the games they played. "Listen," I'd tell them, "I don't bet. I'm not going to play chess with you." It was part of winning respect.

RAMÓN LABAÑINO: I'd like to add something on the question of solidarity. Actually it's not exactly solidarity; it's about the guards. Usually, when we'd get to a new prison—and I was in every type: maximum, medium, and minimum security—the guards would be afraid of us at first. They'd seen our files, which say we were convicted of "conspiracy to commit espionage." You'd feel the tension. But as they got to know us, even the way the officers viewed us began to change.

A big part of that was the solidarity that started coming in from all over. We began to receive newspapers—like the *Militant*—with front-page articles about the Cuban Five and books with photos of us in them. You wouldn't believe how much this helped. It was testimony to the solidarity with us around the world.

The guards would begin to shift. "This guy can't be what it says here in the government file. Somebody is lying. This guy is a hero of the Republic of Cuba!"

Over time some officers took an interest in the case. I remember one who had read something on the website of the International Committee for the Freedom of the Cuban Five, or the National Committee to Free the Cuban Five. I don't remember which. He came to me and said, "Man, you're bad, bad!" *Bad* in the sense that you're *good*.

And I said to myself, "Oh Lord. . . "

Oscar and Carlos Alberto became my compañeros and brothers.

RENÉ GONZÁLEZ: The letters also helped a lot, letters from people around the world. Other prisoners would say, "People really like this man." I remember when postage stamps with our faces were issued. We received them on many letters sent by children in Cuba. Other prisoners would ask me to sign one of the stamps for them. Even prison officers, although they tried not to be seen doing it.

All those things helped.

MARY-ALICE WATERS: Fernando, you were in prison at different times with both Oscar López and Carlos Alberto Torres, the Puerto Rican independence fighters.* That must have been quite an experience.

FERNANDO GONZÁLEZ: In the two prisons where I did most

---

* Oscar López and Carlos Alberto Torres were framed up by the US government and imprisoned for decades. López, who is serving a seventy-year sentence, has been in federal prisons since 1981. Torres was freed on parole in July 2010 after serving thirty years of a seventy-eight-year sentence.

of my time, I was able to share that time with two individuals who were politically conscious revolutionaries sentenced to prison for political reasons. I consider myself privileged.

At the federal prison in Oxford, Wisconsin, for more than five years, I got to know Carlos Alberto Torres, and I spent nearly five years in the Terre Haute, Indiana, prison with Oscar López Rivera. My relationship with them was different from that with other prisoners. You establish good relations with many people, but Oscar and Carlos became my compañeros and brothers.

MARY-ALICE WATERS: Did you share a cell?

FERNANDO GONZÁLEZ: With Carlos Alberto, no. We were in the same unit but not the same cell. Oscar and I shared a cell for some time.

Most prisoners have a relatively low level of political consciousness and interest in political questions. But with these two compañeros I could have a different kind of discussion. They are well-informed compañeros, with solid political education. Our conversations covered many topics, including daily events.

When I got to prison, Oscar and Carlos Alberto each had already been there a long time, and I benefited from their experience. Their view of prison life was different, not the way other prisoners saw things.

That's why I say I felt privileged. It's not just having gotten to know them personally. It's the kind of human beings they are. They are extremely humane and supportive of others. They know the history of Puerto Rico, the struggles of the Puerto Rican people. And both compañeros are also very well informed about Cuba.

Oscar is older. His experiences go back to the struggles of the 1960s and 1970s in the United States. Not only the Puerto Rican independence movement but also struggles by Afri-

SETH GALINSKY/MILITANT

BORICUA HUMAN RIGHTS NETWORK

Top: New York, June 8, 2014. Contingent in Puerto Rican Day parade demands freedom for Oscar López, longest held Puerto Rican independence fighter in US prisons. **Bottom:** Carlos Alberto Torres (in dark shirt), after his release from 30 years in prison, is greeted in San Juan, Puerto Rico, July 2010.

Fernando González shared several years in federal prison with each of the two independence fighters—at Oxford, Wisconsin, with Torres and at Terre Haute, Indiana, with López.

"Oscar and Carlos Alberto are conscious revolutionaries who were sentenced to prison for political reasons. When I got to prison, each had already been there a long time and I benefited from their experience. They became my compañeros and brothers. I consider myself privileged to have known them."
—Fernando González

can Americans, Chicanos, Native Americans, and others that
were part of the radical left.

RÓGER CALERO: Oscar says his political views were pro-
foundly changed by his experience as a young man drafted
into the US army to serve in Vietnam during Washington's
brutal war there.

FERNANDO GONZÁLEZ: When I met Oscar in prison, I went
over and said hello. "Yes, I know who you are"—that's the
first thing he said to me. Remember, we had never met each
other. But he knew about our case, the names of all five of us,
the history of our fight, and a lot about Cuba, too.

Carlos Alberto and Oscar both understood what our case
represented politically. And because of the political education I had received in Cuba about the history of Puerto
Rico—which is so close to that of our own—I could understand perfectly the situation they were in. Within the possi-
bilities at hand, I could contribute to the campaign for their
release.

MARY-ALICE WATERS: The fight to win Oscar's freedom is
gaining momentum, especially with mounting anger among
Puerto Ricans at the economic crisis hitting the island so
hard due to its colonial status. There's a notable increase in
the breadth of forces demanding Oscar's freedom. He was
officially honored by organizers of the Puerto Rican Day parade in New York last year, and again this year there was a
big contingent demanding his freedom.

FERNANDO GONZÁLEZ: If there's anything I would call my
best years in prison—if you can use such an expression, since
I don't wish prison on anyone—it would be those years with
Oscar. It was an exceptional experience.

PART 4

Solidarity worldwide gave us the strength to resist during the worst times

MARY-ALICE WATERS: On the eve of US entry into the Second World War, the entire leadership of the Socialist Workers Party was tried on charges of seditious conspiracy and conspiracy to advocate the overthrow of the US government.

FERNANDO GONZÁLEZ: Seditious conspiracy—that's the same charge used against Oscar López.

MARY-ALICE WATERS: Yes. The SWP leaders were convicted and imprisoned on the second charge. They were sentenced December 8, 1941, the day after the Japanese military's attack on the US naval base at Pearl Harbor in Hawaii. The central leaders of the party and of the Teamster union organizing drive across the Upper Midwest were sentenced to sixteen months at what was perhaps the most politically charged moment of the US imperialist war drive.

I mention the length of the sentences, because it's a striking counterpoint to the sentences you and many others have received in recent years. It tells you something about the evolution of the US "justice" system.

Fourteen of the eighteen comrades were able to serve their sentences together, in the same prison. They could communicate with each other, support each other. And they used the time to do what revolutionary leaders often have a hard time accomplishing amid all the demands of leadership in the class struggle: to organize serious reading and study. Jim Cannon—a founding leader of the communist movement in the US, and one of those railroaded to prison—referred to it as his "semester at Sandstone University . . ."

FERNANDO GONZÁLEZ: As in Sandstone, Minnesota?

MARY-ALICE WATERS: Yes, they were sent to the federal prison in Sandstone.

All of you are also well acquainted with the Abel Santamaría Academy that Fidel and the other Moncada combatants organized during the year and a half they were imprisoned on the Isle of Pines. You didn't have the same kind of opportunity, since you were sent to five distant prisons. But we know from your letters, from the books you asked for and received from many places, and from the comments you made about the things you were reading, that study was a crucial part of your lives.

How important was this for you in prison? And how did your drawing, painting, and poetry become a form of resistance? As Fernando said in a recent interview, he used 20 per cent of his time to follow what was going on inside the prison and 80 per cent to follow what was going on in the world.

FERNANDO GONZÁLEZ: In prison, after I'd gotten used to the surroundings, I promised myself that I'd use the time for my own benefit, that I'd leave with my mental and physical health intact. If I had failed on that, they would have won the fight.

I spent a lot of time reading, and that gave me an advantage. I told myself over and over that just because I was passing through prison, I didn't have to become a "prisoner."

ANTONIO GUERRERO: It was a process of self-improvement, on top of the education we already had. There are millions of books, many of which are easy to read and entertaining. It seems sometimes in prison that you have all the time in the world, although at another level you know that's not true. Self-improvement is only possible through reading and learning from others. And the results you get depend on the choices you make.

We read a wide variety of things, which came to us by many different routes. The other day we were with a compañero from Puerto Rico at an event in eastern Cuba—it was July 26, when we climbed Turquino Peak. For a whole period that compañero sent each of us Fidel's "Reflections," which have been printed in the newspapers and online in Cuba.

We also received a news bulletin from the Cuban Interests Section in Washington. It was very valuable, despite the delays in getting it. It carried national and international news, with a focus on issues related to Cuba. I'd spend days reading it in my bunk.

Later it became possible for us to receive e-mail in prison, and compañeros could send us at least the most important news, two or three e-mails a day. We had such good sources of information that we didn't watch television.

Except when we were in the hole and had to read whatever we could get our hands on, we also had the privilege of receiving your books, good books that, as Martí said, you get something out of. That opportunity is much more limited for the vast majority of prisoners, of course.

I read a lot of the books I received. Others I ended up having to send to Cuba because of the "shakedowns." Prison officials would sometimes tell us we had too many books, that we had to get rid of them. Or when I was transferred, I had boxes of books I couldn't take with me.

Personally I spent a lot of time reading poetry and art books. The only way I could learn how to paint with watercolors, and then with pastels and oil, was by reading. The more I read, the more I wanted to read, including books from museums. I enjoyed all the poetry I came across. I studied chess; I had a big, thick book of chess problems. I have it here in Cuba, in my house. Often I'd lie in bed working them out.

Books that helped us grow
René González

Not a week went by that we didn't receive the *Militant* with something about the Five in it. Getting out word about the cause, defending us. . . .

In prison, the books by Pathfinder helped us grow, helped us see the world, helped us become more Marxist. In an environment where all you saw on television was inanities, you could shut yourself up in your cell, grab a Pathfinder book, and you were in another world. You were learning, analyzing, maturing, becoming a better person.

The *Militant* would slip its way through the prison. My friends would sneak it into the library. It would be removed and they'd slip it back in. A real struggle was waged so that people could read Pathfinder literature, and read it they did.

HAVANA INTERNATIONAL BOOK FAIR
FEBRUARY 2014

The important thing was not just having a source of books, but the energy and time to read things that are useful. I think we succeeded in that. And it had an influence on other people.

I read a wide range of novels, too, including ones like *The Da Vinci Code*. Sometimes a book lists other titles by the same author—by Dan Brown, in that case—and you try to get them all. Until at a certain point you get bored and ask yourself, why am I reading this? Because you know you're not getting anything from them.

We also received the magazine *Bohemia*, mailed direct from Cuba. And the Cuban publications you sent us, as well, including *Granma International* and *La Gaceta de Cuba*, the magazine of the National Union of Writers and Artists of Cuba.

RAMÓN LABAÑINO: *Temas* magazine too. I like it a lot. The articles on the Cuban economy in *Temas* are very controversial.

ANTONIO GUERRERO: We were practically a minilibrary—a minilibrary of good materials that we often passed on to others.

There were Cubans with whom we walked, shared books and other things. But their view of the world was often far from ours. Sometimes you'd just say to yourself, "I'm not going to get into a confrontation with this guy, because I can't change his way of thinking." They respected me, I respected them. I listened to them.

As Fernando said, we didn't have the good fortune of being with our compañeros. But we did have the good fortune of continually receiving publications, and their number increased as solidarity work grew. That gave us a level of information we considered a great privilege.

GERARDO HERNÁNDEZ: I saw the movement in solidarity with our fight as a great big machine made up of many small parts, so if one failed another kept working. The outcome last December was due to very specific facts. It had to do with the year and a half of negotiations between the US and Cuban governments, which are now public.

But our release would never have been possible without the work over many years by thousands of ordinary people who publicized our case.

Just ask yourself, why would the US government have needed to release the Five if nobody knew who we were? Why would Washington bother, if people weren't continually demanding our freedom? We can't underestimate the impact of all these efforts over the years. Our release was the result of broad, united solidarity efforts.

This solidarity was essential to our own day-to-day resistance, too.

When they put me in "the box" at Lompoc in 2003, for example, I learned that friends were demonstrating at the Bureau of Prisons and Department of Justice in Washington, with signs demanding our freedom. That gave me tremendous strength. I told myself: my job in this small space is to resist—not to get a panic attack and give up. My mission is to add to the efforts of so many friends outside. If they could do that in the rain or in hot weather, taking time off from their jobs, how could I not do my part too?

> ### Books by Malcolm X flew out of my hands. They are gold in prison. Books about Martin Luther King, too.

People sometimes don't talk about this. But the value of solidarity can be seen in the results. And I have to stress how important it was for us during the worst times in prison.

RAMÓN LABAÑINO: The books we received were very important in that regard. I had a long line of people waiting for them. The day I received *Cuba and Angola*, with all the photos from the struggle against the South African apartheid regime in Angola on the cover, it caused a sensation.[*] Most US Blacks in the prison population didn't know Cuban volunteers had been in Angola for sixteen years, defending its sovereignty

---

[*] *Cuba and Angola: Fighting for Africa's Freedom and Our Own* by Fidel Castro, Raúl Castro, Nelson Mandela, and others (Pathfinder Press, 2013).

Top: (from right) Gerardo Hernández, Fernando González, Antonio Guerrero, Ramón Labañino, and René González in Caracas, Venezuela, May 2015. **Bottom:** Arrival in South Africa, June 2015. During the year following their return to Cuba in December 2014, the Five together visited more than half a dozen countries in Latin America and Africa to thank supporters of their fight for freedom and extend solidarity to other struggles.

"Our release would never have been possible without the work over many years by thousands of ordinary people who publicized our case." *—Gerardo Hernández*

Top: Baltimore, April 23, 2015. Unionists and others demand prosecution of cops responsible for the death in police custody of Freddie Gray. **Bottom:** Chicago, November 10, 2015, march by fast-food workers and others for $15 an hour and a union, part of national day of actions.

"People murdered by the police. McDonald's and other workers demanding higher wages. Walmart in trouble. This is the real United States."
—*Ramón Labañino*

against South Africa. The system of disinformation in the United States erases history.

What Cuba did in Angola was decisive in the struggle against apartheid and for the final liberation of Namibia, Angola, and South Africa. But that isn't well known in the United States. So there was a long waiting list for that book.

When I received books, I'd read them and then immediately pass them on. Afterward I'd sit down with others to talk about them. Two or three would read a book and then they'd say, "Hey, come out this afternoon, let's sit outside." And we'd start to discuss and debate. Both Americans and Cubans.

None of this was planned. I would explain my point of view, and the others would explain theirs. One of them, a former university professor, had a totally imperialist mindset. When I knew I had his trust, I told him that. "You're an imperialist, *chico*! You have an imperialist mentality."

These debates were like political discussion circles. I'd present the facts. When I explained why Cuban troops went to Angola, it had an impact.

Books by Malcolm X flew out of my hands. I couldn't hold onto them—they are gold in prison. Books about Martin Luther King, too. You never got them back, because people kept passing them from one to another to another. Books by Fidel, biographies of Cuban revolutionaries, the *Militant* and all the other newspapers we were getting—I couldn't keep my hands on them.

I'd say to someone: read these articles and then tell me what TV station gives you information about these things happening in the United States? This is the real United States, here in the *Militant*. Strikes. People murdered by the police. Fights for pay increases. Why McDonald's workers are demanding higher wages. Why Walmart is in trouble. This is what's happening in the United States.

It's difficult to get news in prison. The television is almost always tuned to MTV. Hip-hop music is what's most popular. It's not that you like CNN, but at least they show a little news. Even Fox. But most people want music in the morning and the latest movies.

Reading these things in the *Militant* had an impact. It became the starting point of conversations, like links in a chain. They'd ask to take pictures of us together to send to their families. Then the families would want us to send them books. I hope you keep sending the *Militant* and books to the prisons, because they educate people.

We also received a scientific magazine called *Mar y Pesca* [Ocean and Fishing]. It would barely last five minutes in my hands. And when I started getting youth and humor magazines from Cuba—*Somos Jóvenes*, *Zunzún*, *Pionero*, and *Dedeté*—other Cubans took them right out of my hands too.

GERARDO HERNÁNDEZ: *Granma International* was also very important in providing information about Cuba.

It's one thing to sit with a prisoner and begin to talk about Cuba, the situation in the United States, or the case of the Five. But it's a lot easier to say, "Look, study this newspaper or this book and then let's talk." And we were able to do that. People would tell us: "I didn't know this was happening in my country, right here in the US." Or "I didn't know there were parties besides the Democrats and Republicans." They used to tell us that.

I'm not saying this because we're talking to you now. It's important to call attention to the work by Pathfinder during our years in prison. That support continued from the beginning of the battle for our liberation until the last day.

You know, just yesterday I received a letter from one of the people I'd share the *Militant* and other publications with. Everyone called him Zacatecas, but his name is Norberto Quin-

Cuba and the Coming American Revolution

Ramón Labañino

I just read *Playa Girón*, and I can't tell you how much I liked it. I've read a lot on this important event in Cuba's history, but I was struck by a detail I can't ignore:

The preface by Jack Barnes explains the Cuban Revolution's direct example and impact on the people of the US and on the revolutionary left and movement in solidarity with our country. It describes the impact of the battle [against the US-backed invading forces at the Bay of Pigs in April 1961] and the defeat of the mercenary force at Playa Girón on US students, intellectuals, and the progressive movement. It describes the struggle in the US against the government, its lies, its propaganda machine, always at the service of the rich and powerful....

This was something I'd never read anywhere else.

LETTER TO PATHFINDER PRESS
JULY 14, 2002

tana. You know what he wrote? "Since you left, we've missed those publications," he said. "We miss the *Militant*."

FERNANDO GONZÁLEZ: The prisons each of us passed through had libraries filled with Pathfinder books. One of the funniest things was that I'd get a Pathfinder book, read it, pass it on to someone, that person would pass it on to somebody else and so on, and in the end. . .

GERARDO HERNÁNDEZ: It would come back to you.

FERNANDO GONZÁLEZ: No, it would wind up in the library. Then a couple of months later someone would come to me and say, "Hey Cuba, there's a book in the library you'll really like!"

RAMÓN LABAÑINO: There's another book that people also read a lot—the book by Jack Barnes, *Cuba and the Coming American Revolution*.

MARY-ALICE WATERS: I remember the letter you sent us after reading the introduction by Jack Barnes to *Playa Girón/Bay of Pigs: Washington's First Military Defeat in the Americas*. It was later included in *Cuba and the Coming American Revolution*, as well.

RAMÓN LABAÑINO: And there was the book you sent us about the three Chinese Cuban generals, too, *Our History Is Still Being Written*. Other Cubans wanted to take it from me as soon as they saw it.

> "We've met with Cubans across the country. And it's really a sharing of views. We learn from them."
> —*Fernando González*

LISANDRA CARDOSO/RADIO ANGULO

Holguín: Ramón Labañino (third from left) at KTP combine factory, December 2015. "We owe our freedom to international solidarity and to men and women like you who fought without letup," Labañino told a gathering of workers from this and a nearby plant.

RODNY ALCOLEA OLIVARES/TRABAJADORES

Guantánamo: René González with students and teachers at medical school, October 2014. They peppered him with questions about his experiences as an internationalist volunteer combatant in Angola in 1977–79, his years in Miami monitoring counterrevolutionary groups, and what the Five faced in US prisons.

> "We tell people to be prepared but not afraid. And we start with a great strength: a people who are politically educated and ready for these challenges."
>
> —*Ramón Labañino*

PHOTOS BY LIXANDER CRUZ/RADIO JUVENIL

Calixto García: Fernando González (plaid shirt) in rural eastern town, December 2015. Farmers tilling previously idle land told him of their efforts to boost food production.

RAMÓN FRONTERA

Turquino Peak: The Five after climbing highest mountain in Cuba, July 2015. "Already during our first days in the 'hole' we talked about the day we would celebrate together at the top of Turquino," René González said. "We fulfilled that promise." They invited Puerto Rican independence fighters Malcolm Frontera (in dark shirt) and his father, Ramón Frontera (photographer), to join them in a show of support for fight to free Oscar López.

Havana: René González addresses national congress of Federation of University Students (FEU), June 2013. "We must understand why it's necessary for capitalism to disappear as a system," he said. He urged students to "go beyond the classroom…. We can't forget that many young people aren't in school, but they produce the wealth with their hands."

Havana: Gerardo Hernández at event in Arroyo Naranjo neighborhood where he grew up, March 2015. As 55 teenagers were admitted as members of local Committee in Defense of the Revolution (CDR), he said, "Don't view your membership card as a mere formality, but as an important commitment, because Cuba needs its youth as never before."

"Who got us out of the Special Period? We must give credit to the young people: those serving as doctors in other countries, building hotels here, going back to rural areas to farm. They have defended socialism under the leadership of the revolution." —*Antonio Guerrero*

Camagüey: Tony Guerrero (above, white shirt) with students at University of Camagüey in central Cuba. He learned about projects by engineering students to build experimental housing and (right) joined students in simultaneous chess matches.

PHOTOS BY MIOZOTIS FABELO/RADIO REBELDE

ISMAEL FRANCISCO/CUBADEBATE

Havana: Cuban Five in lead contingent of million-strong 2015 May Day march. As much as the capitalist media abroad "wants to hide the reality of Cuba, they can't hide millions of revolutionaries in the street," said Gerardo Hernández.

PART 5

We're in a battle of ideas and we intend to win

MARY-ALICE WATERS: Up to now we've been talking about your experiences as part of the working class in the United States. Before we end, let's talk about your lives and responsibilities since December 17, 2014, when you were all reunited here in Cuba.

Washington's decision to release Gerardo, Ramón, and Antonio and reestablish diplomatic relations with the Cuban government was a recognition that the policies carried out by eleven consecutive US administrations—Democratic and Republican alike, from Dwight Eisenhower to Barack Obama—failed to achieve their objective. That's a tribute to decades of resistance by the Cuban people, a tremendous victory.

But Washington's objective hasn't changed, just the methods. The goal remains to overturn the transformed property and social relations conquered in revolutionary struggle in Cuba more than fifty years ago, and to reestablish the rule of capital. The US economic war against Cuba has not ended. Washington continues to occupy Cuba's sovereign territory at Guantánamo Bay. Millions of dollars each year continue to be poured into US government-funded programs aimed at "regime change."

Washington's new tactics bring new challenges, however. Since your release, you've traveled to virtually every cor-

ner of the island, exchanging views with many thousands
of Cubans, especially young people. Coming out of all these
discussions, how do you see the challenges ahead?

FERNANDO GONZÁLEZ: We've had dozens of meetings, in
provinces across Cuba, like the one you were part of last February at CUJAE, the main science and technology university
here in Havana. We always give priority to exchanges with
students and young workers. And it really is a sharing of
views. We learn from them.

One place I visited was Cabo de San Antonio, at the west-
ernmost tip of Cuba. I met with a unit of border guards sta-
tioned in a remote area, a very inhospitable spot. They were
recruits, ten or twelve young men about eighteen or nineteen
years old, with two officers who were a few years older. They
were carrying out a difficult assignment, guarding the coast
and looking for drug smugglers. They're an example of the
young people we meet.

There are always those in the older generations who say,
"Young people today are lost." When I was young I remember people grumbling, "Ah, the youth today!" Yes, there are
always young people who part their hair a different way or
dye it various colors.

RAMÓN LABAÑINO: And there always will be.

FERNANDO GONZÁLEZ: But what I see wherever I've gone are
young people who are learning from experience. Education
never ends.

RAMÓN LABAÑINO: Wherever we visit, and not only here,
we're asked about the future of Cuba, about relations with
the United States. It's a constant concern.

Whenever we meet with young people, we feel a huge responsibility to communicate with them. Because expectations are high.

The goal of US imperialism continues to be to restore its

domination of Cuba. That's the fact. It's no accident that the first businesses the US government wants to set up here are telecommunications networks. We'll also see businesses from the US trying to "buy brains" here, as they do all over the world. They'll try to transform us into a capitalist economy. That's their aim.

> *US imperialism's goal is to restore its domination of Cuba. They want to transform us into a capitalist economy.*

We need to confront these new relations with the United States with our eyes wide open, and that's what we explain to young people.

FERNANDO GONZÁLEZ: We know Washington's intentions. Obama says the results of previous US policy were a failure. So, as you said, the US government is going to use new tactics against us. They're still trying to figure out how to strangle Cuba.

But we continue to stand up to them. Obviously Cubans want to be able to move forward, to have a better life. We want relations with the United States, the more respectful the better. We never forget, however, that while they greet us with smiles on their faces at summit conferences, or at embassy cocktail parties, their intention is still to cut off our heads. That hasn't changed.

We're in a battle of ideas, and we intend to win.

RAMÓN LABAÑINO: Yes, that's our main struggle. Helping to open people's eyes. Telling them to be prepared but not afraid. And we start with a very great strength—with youth and a people who are politically educated, who are ready for these challenges.

We are living through a historic moment in which we have to make changes to ensure our own survival. But no one should have any doubts that we are a people with dignity who know how to defend our sovereignty. And that we and our leaders are prepared to face adversity in the difficult fights ahead.

RENÉ GONZÁLEZ: The Cuba we found on our return has had to adapt to a capitalist world, which for nearly three decades we'd been able to keep at arm's length thanks to the existence of a socialist camp. Suddenly, in 1989, the country found itself in a new situation, like a small ship adrift in a big storm. We had to swing the wheel hard and do so without veering off our course, which is to build socialism.

We've had to do things that, because of the values we're educated in, we don't like to do. But history is like that. It lets us take a few steps forward, as Lenin said, and then makes us take some backward too. We have resisted quite successfully since the fall of the USSR.

I think the changes we're making are correct. What results from them depends on us. A door has been opened by the beginning of normalization of relations with the US government, but this also brings a set of serious challenges. If we can overcome these challenges, we will move faster toward socialism.

GERARDO HERNÁNDEZ: The Cuba we came back to is a different Cuba. That didn't surprise me, since we stayed quite well informed of what was going on. We find a Cuba with many good things, as well as some negative developments, things that didn't exist before. But I still see a people ready to keep fighting to overcome the challenges imposed by our enemies.

There are some who say the current economic and social reforms are a step toward capitalism. In some cases, that's because it's what they want to see happen, in my opinion.

FERNANDO GONZÁLEZ: There are certain sections of the left who fear we're headed toward restoring capitalism. I thought Abel Prieto answered them quite well earlier this year, when he said, "Marx never said gas stations have to be state-owned." It's the means of production that have to be state-owned. That's what decides who is really in power.

RAMÓN LABAÑINO: What we're explaining here also needs to be understood by some compañeros on the left. I saw a headline in a left-wing German newspaper the other day warning us, "Cuba, Don't Trust the United States." The truth is, that's been our watchword for a long time. It was Che Guevara who said, "We never trust imperialism, not even a tiny bit!"

RÓGER CALERO: Yes, I've seen the film clip of Che saying that. I remember him squinching his thumb and forefinger together as he emphasized, "not even a tiny bit."

GERARDO HERNÁNDEZ: We face what is virtually a new world, but I'm convinced there are many Cubans who will fight so we never return to the pre-1959 Cuba. Who will fight the abysmal inequality that exists in many countries, where the powerful crush the needy.

To go back to the old Cuba would be to deny our history and the sacrifices made by so many who have died to prevent that from happening.

The future of our revolution, the future of our homeland, is in the hands of the youth we've been exchanging views with over the months since we returned to Cuba. We've been learning about their concerns, what they're thinking, what they're worried about.

As Fernando said, there's a tendency among some to think young people today have run off the rails, to think that they're lost. To some extent, that happens with every generation. Perhaps it's more noticeable because of the many challenges our country is facing right now.

At the opening of the 1990s, not only did our trade and other economic relations with the Soviet Union collapse, but the US government also tightened the blockade. The Special Period our country went through during those difficult years had a negative impact on some of our social values—that's no secret to anyone. But it's also true that our youth embody many positive values. I'm optimistic, because we've gotten to know them. The future of the revolution is safe.

I just returned from Camagüey, where we talked to some young people we ran into at the beach. Some of them had long hair, countless nose rings, rings in their ears. They came to say hello. As we began to talk, we learned that among them were national vanguard youth, student leaders, members of the Union of Young Communists. There were even members of the party.

You can't just go by appearances. We heard so many stories of young people who have climbed Turquino Peak five, six, seven times, who have spent their vacations doing voluntary work.

For our part, as the soldiers we are, we've scarcely had a moment of rest since we returned. This is supposed to be a bit of a break while we're waiting for the new tasks we'll be asked to shoulder. Meanwhile, we've been making our small contribution, adding our grain of sand to keep the revolution moving forward.

ANTONIO GUERRERO: We shouldn't forget that the youth we're talking about are our sons and daughters, and the generation coming right behind them. I left Cuba in 1991 at the beginning of the worst years of the Special Period, when we were going through a wrenching change in our economic situation. Store shelves were empty. Food and gasoline were scarce.

Now we come back in 2014 and see that things are different. Today you go to a store—and yes, you have to have dollar-convertible pesos—but you find things on the shelves. There are little private restaurants, what we call a *paladar*. Some people have left Cuba, to go here or there. The situation is not even remotely like what we faced in the first half of the 1990s, however. The world we live in has shifted, and we had to shift.

When I think about young people in Cuba today, I ask myself a simple question: Who produced everything that got us out of that crisis? We have to give credit to the young people who went through that period. We have to acknowledge what they've built.

Where are they working today? How many countries are our young doctors and teachers serving in? Who is producing all the medicine and building all the hotels here? Who is going back to rural areas to farm today? We have to recognize that young people in Cuba have shown themselves capable of doing all these things—that they've made it all the way here defending the revolution.

And under whose leadership? Under the historic leadership of the revolution, defending socialism.

The empire wants to impose a change in our political system and values. Sometimes they work to do so very subtly. But our revolutionary ideology calls for sacrifice. That's not sloganeering—it's what we talked about with the students at CUJAE. It's something real.

But, clearly, as Fernando said, we're living in different times. All the material things, the Internet. We see it in our children.

It influences us too. To be a revolutionary you have to weigh these things and be willing to contribute your share of sacrifice. And to this day, many of the youth in Cuba still hold these values.

The problems we see young people facing when we go around the world are very different from the problems Cuban youth are confronting. Our revolutionary struggle has already resolved a million problems young people elsewhere face.

The challenge confronting young people in Cuba, the challenge confronting all of us here, is to help develop the values of the most important struggle facing humankind—the struggle against putting yourself first. That's the point of the battle of ideas. We need to explain things in a way that someone we're talking with can say: "Well, this guy said only a few words, but he's backed up what he said in action, and he continues to do so."

That's why Fidel's example has endured: it has been consistent.

I want to say something about Guantánamo. Mary-Alice mentioned that Cuban territory was seized from us more than a century ago. The treaty establishing a US naval coaling station at Guantánamo Bay was signed by a Cuban president who had been imposed on us by Washington. The treaty was supposed to be valid only if both parties agreed on it. Cuba's position has been clear for decades. We are opposed to US occupation of our sovereign territory.

Now there's an additional question: the prison Washington established there in January 2002. Cubans are outraged that something so terrible—something so horrible I can't put a name on it—is being done in our territory. Think about those human beings who've been imprisoned there year after year, without even a trial.

Sometimes you think that what happened to you was the worst. Then you realize it's not. It's nothing compared to what has happened to other human beings.

You have to feel the injustice in your bones, no matter where it's being committed, as Che used to say. That's what Guantánamo is—the most unjust link in the chain of imperial "justice."

RAMÓN LABAÑINO: Let me add one final thing. We need to congratulate the Cuban people, because Cuba hasn't given an inch in our revolutionary principles. It was the US government that had to say, "We're going to change our methods, because they haven't worked."

We should feel very proud and optimistic. Because we've won a moral victory. We won it through resistance, sacrifice, and loyalty.

Fidel showed us the road, and we defended it with our blood, weapons in hand. And that's the road we continue to defend.

We will take our place in
the trenches and be judged
by the work we do

We lived in a microcosm of the outside world

GERARDO HERNÁNDEZ

The following interview by Cuban journalists Yosbel Bullaín Viltres and Yuliat Danay Acosta appeared in the online publication *Cubadebate*. It was published on July 26, 2015, the anniversary of the historic attacks on the dictatorship's army garrisons in Santiago de Cuba and Bayamo in 1953 led by Fidel Castro. That was the opening battle of the revolutionary struggle in Cuba that five and a half years later, on January 1, 1959, brought down the US-backed tyranny of Fulgencio Batista.

■

Peace is vitally important to Gerardo Hernández. Only those who've been deprived of natural light and contact with their loved ones as a result of risking their lives to defend the lives of others can appreciate the value of a safe, peaceful environment.

This Sunday, Gerardo will have a second chance to experience something as though for the very first time. After more than sixteen years in prison, he will once again be able to celebrate July 26 with his loved ones. But his memories remain intact, like a photo album in chronological order. It's impossible to erase what you have lived.

On behalf of the Five, Gerardo spoke to Cubadebate *about why he defends his ideas and how, in personally symbolic ways, they celebrated from afar the Cuban Revolution's historic dates. He also spoke about how, even in prison, those who live in the United States cannot escape the manipulation in the press that Cuba is subjected to on such occasions.*

In addition to the regular punishment that imprisonment implies, we faced a few additional abuses. One of them was that if we felt like watching television, we had to suffer through the same propaganda that everyone in the United States lives with. For example, on May 20, [the Spanish-language network] Univision in particular would broadcast its congratulations to Cuba on its Independence Day![*] And sometimes prisoners would hear that and turn around and say to me, "Hey Cuba, congratulations!"

And I'd say to them, "Don't congratulate me today; I'm not celebrating yet!"

"But why?"

And then I'd have to explain: "January 1 is when you should congratulate me!"

These were great opportunities for a history lesson, because they were congratulating me in good faith. It happened constantly: "Congratulations, Cuba! Congratulations!"

---

[*] Opponents of the 1959 revolution celebrate May 20, 1902, as Cuba's independence day. That was the date the first elected president took office in Cuba. Four years earlier, however, US government troops had invaded Cuba. The Spanish armed forces, on the verge of defeat at the hands of Cuban freedom fighters, surrendered to the US army in July 1898. Washington put the island under military occupation and in 1901 imposed the so-called Platt Amendment on Cuba's constitution, affirming the US government's "right to intervene" at will in Cuba. Thus, the 1902 declaration of Cuba's formal "independence" masked the reality of US imperialist domination, including the 1903 "treaty" sanctifying Washington's seizure of Cuban territory at Guantánamo Bay—one of the best natural harbors in the world—for a US naval base.

On July 26, of course, the vast majority of the television channels never so much as mentioned the date, although at times on
some of the English-language channels something appeared,
especially if there was a very large rally in Cuba. They would
refer to the date and explain a little, in very broad strokes. And
I would always wear my little Cuban flag pin, which I still have,
because I was able to bring it back. In fact, I wore it quite often, even if there was no historic date to celebrate. But I always
wore it for our important national dates and celebrations.

Whenever I wore it, people would notice and say to me,
"Hey Cuba, you're all dressed up today!"

"No," I'd explain, "it's because today's an important day."
And so that was how it was on January 1, on Fidel's birthday,
on July 26—our historic dates. This was our way of commem-
orating them, because there was no other way to do it.

These incidents gave us the opportunity to educate many
people about these questions. As the years passed, people
with whom we'd been together for a long time already understood. And, it goes without saying, the same was true about
our case. We always used our case as an example when we
spoke with the other prisoners.

The media also painted prerevolutionary Cuba as a heaven
on earth. In response, I'd tell this story. When I was still free, I
listened to Miami radio stations to keep tabs on Radio Mambí.
One day, a woman called in to one of these talk shows and
said:

"Oh Martha, those communists with their claims! It's all a
lie, Martha! Because I remember, Martha, we had a yacht and
we lived in Miramar and we used to go down to the yacht and
go out sailing on those lovely Cuban afternoons. And all
that about people being taken prisoner and being tortured, all
lies, Martha! If you knew someone in the government, they'd
get you out, Martha."

January 1959. Page from widely circulated Cuban weekly magazine *Bohemia* shows instruments of torture found in a police station when military dictatorship was overthrown. "Torture chamber in Santa Clara: Incredible cruelty of the tyranny," headline says.

When other prisoners asked why officials of the Batista dictatorship were tried and some were executed in the months following the victory, "I told them about the kinds of things that were found in police stations after the revolution—with every kind of torture instrument imaginable, even implements for gouging out eyes." *—Gerardo Hernández*

And I'd say to myself, "What unbelievable things this woman is saying!"

When someone had confidence in you, he'd ask, "Is that how it was? People were just sent to the firing squad?"

I had to explain the kinds of things that we found in the police stations after the revolution—every kind of torture instrument imaginable, even implements for gouging out eyes.

Nobody can imagine these kinds of things, much less Cubans! For a young man, it's not easy to absorb. You need time to let it sink in. Those issues of *Bohemia* magazine with pictures of young people who'd been murdered—tortured and thrown into a pond with a pipe bomb fastened around their chest. And the dictatorship said these youths were the terrorists. Those things had a deep impact on me!

When you get to the US, they show photos of those shot by firing squads after the dictatorship was overthrown and go on and on about those executed by Castro, by Che. One of the pictures they always show is a famous one of Cornelio Rojas, who was, I believe, chief of police in Santa Clara. I remember he was wearing a white suit. When he was shot, *Bohemia* said his last words were, "Okay, you boys got this far. Keep moving forward with the revolution!"

And the guy was a ruthless murderer!

So they show the photo of his execution, when he falls into a pit. They show photos of men tried and executed by "Castro's firing squads," but they never tell you who that man really was. When they'd show a documentary like that, I'd say to the young prisoners: "Yes he was shot, but who was that man?" And I'd tell them about all the torture devices that were found in the police stations.

Afterwards, when we received the book *Desde la soledad y la esperanza* [Between Solitude and Hope] from Cuba—the

book containing works by various artists about our case—
there was a section that included the photos from *Bohemia*
showing those instruments for removing fingernails or eyes.
"Look here," I'd say, "this is the Cuba that they want you to
think was a paradise!"

> *The last cellmate I had was a young man,*
> *twenty-four years old,*
> *who was serving a double life sentence.*

I think this history is something we need to stress, because today, when I speak with my nephews, for example,
they've never seen these photos. We have to continue to
stress this, so that people know what really happened here.
The cars, architecture, and music of the 1950s are in fashion today, but nobody is talking about the other things that
happened here in the fifties. We have to continue to remind
young people of that. If we don't, if we let those who por-
tray those years as Cuba's golden age win the battle, we'll
be in bad shape.

For example, at my old high school, former Police Station
no. 14, I'm sure many of the students today don't really know
what happened there before, or how many young people
were tortured in the basement where they now take shop
classes. We've got to constantly explain things like that, otherwise it's just another school, just another building. But every place has its history.

How many times do we pass by a plaque without anyone
stopping to look at it? On that very street corner, a student
might have been shot and killed, yet people pass without no-

ticing. That's because we were born into a peaceful country, a country where such crimes don't occur.

The five of us spent sixteen years together with young people from Mexico, El Salvador, Honduras, the United States, listening to their stories. The last cellmate I had was a young man, twenty-four years old, who was serving a double life sentence.

"Cuba," he told me, "what happened is that I grew up in this environment. My dad had to join the gangs in order to support my family. I grew up seeing that. One day some pickup trucks arrived at my house. They were looking for my dad but he found a place to hide. They took my uncle, and the next morning he'd been killed.

"That divided my family forever. My grandmother never forgave my father. She said it was his fault my uncle had been killed.

"But that's how it is," he told me. "In that city, when you go out with your girlfriend, you have to be very careful. If you pass the wrong place and someone says to you, 'I like that girl,' she will be snatched from your hands. You'll never see her again."

I remember the first time he told me that story, I naively asked him: "But can't you go to the police and file a complaint against them?"

After he stopped laughing at my question, he answered, "The police *work* for them."

That's an example from a Latin American country, but in the United States it's similar. I was sent to the maximum-security prison closest to Los Angeles. The cream of the crop of the Los Angeles gangs end up there. They'd be your cellmates, and you'd hear the stories. They'd talk about the 37th Street gang . . . the 41st Street gang . . . the gang from wherever. If you crossed into the territory of one of these gangs and weren't from there, you'd get shot.

They've been in that environment since they were born. Sometimes I'd talk with them, wondering what circumstances brought a twenty-four-year-old to a maximum-security prison with two life sentences.

Here a child can play until dawn on a street corner near his home and nothing will happen to him.

They'd say to me, "Look Cuba, the problem is that when you go to elementary school here, you have two choices—either you're in a gang or you're abused by the gangs. It's better to be a gang member than to be abused by a gang. And after you enter that world, one day someone puts a gun in your hand and tells you to go kill so-and-so over there. You have to do it because if you don't, they'll kill you."

When people talk about the achievements of the revolution, Cuba's health care and education are internationally recognized. But hardly anything is ever mentioned about the tranquility of our everyday life, the safety we enjoy here, the fact that a child can play until dawn on a street corner near his home and nothing will happen to him. That any tourist can go into the very roughest neighborhood and the worst that will happen is that someone will snatch their gold chain or pull a knife on them and say, "Give me your money." But in any of these other countries, a stray bullet could kill you in broad daylight!

In prison, we lived in a microcosm of that world. You went into the dining room and the African Americans were sitting on one side, some of the Hispanics on another. But watch out, don't make the mistake of sitting at a table that's not for you. If you do, you're looking for trouble. It was that way in the exercise yard too. It's a reflection of society itself: Blacks in one neighborhood, whites in another.

In spite of all of our problems in Cuba, we have the enormous privilege of living in a society that doesn't yet suffer from these evils and, I hope, never will. We have to do whatever it takes to prevent that from happening here. We also have to educate young people, so they understand this privilege we enjoy. They were born with it. The majority haven't experienced the other reality. They take what they have for granted. They believe it's like this everywhere. They don't value it. That's why we have to keep raising the level of consciousness.

In that sense, prison was a tremendous school for us. As I said, we lived in a microcosm of the outside world. We came to know the problems of many places around the world, problems that, unfortunately, are common to many countries.

We're victims of the big-business media. We're victims of the empire's giant publicity machine, which it uses to highlight whatever it finds convenient: nonsense, banalities. We're bombarded by the empire's publicity machine twenty-four hours a day, and, unfortunately, there are people who believe that's all there is. That capitalism is a house with two cars and a swimming pool. That Haiti isn't capitalism. Central America isn't capitalism. The poor neighborhoods of the United States aren't capitalism. Capitalism is whatever it suits them to show!

The battle of ideas is the great battle that we must take up with young people. We have to engage in that battle. If we've done this in other areas, how can we not carry it out on the ideological plane, something that is so important, especially now. Because on the positive side, we're probably going to see a huge influx of tourists. On the negative side, there will also be a lot of people spouting how great things are in the US, or at least what they want people to believe about what it's like there.

For our people, July 26, this historic date, marks the successful struggle that culminated with our tremendous victory in 1959. We're finding that wherever we go—as we walk through the streets, as we visit schools—it's common for fellow Cubans to tell us, "Thank you for what you did for Cuba." But we're also conscious that we, too, have to be grateful.

Behind this victory stand many anonymous heroes who worked hard morning, noon, and night—including many sleepless nights—so the Five could be here to celebrate July 26 along with our people and experience these moments of happiness.

No battle waged
by revolutionaries ends
with what you once did

ANTONIO GUERRERO, RENÉ GONZÁLEZ,
FERNANDO GONZÁLEZ

Gerardo, Ramón, Antonio, Fernando, and René have criss-crossed Cuba multiple times since December 2014, exchanging views almost daily with groups of Cubans in schools and facto-ries, military centers, prisons, and neighborhoods. One of many such events was a meeting February 19, 2015, at Havana's main engineering and science university, popularly known as CUJAE (Ciudad Universitaria "José Antonio Echeverría"). There Antonio, René, and Fernando held a lively exchange with three hundred students, professors, and workers.

The meeting, which took place as the annual Havana Interna-tional Book Fair was under way, included a presentation of *Absolved by Solidarity* by Antonio Guerrero. The book, published by Pathfinder Press, reproduces a set of sixteen watercolors that Guerrero painted in 2014 while he was still in the federal prison in Marianna, Florida. They depict Washington's frame-up trial of the Five.

Also on the speakers platform were Mary-Alice Waters, editor of *Absolved by Solidarity*; university rector Alicia Alonso; and pro-fessor Julián Gutiérrez, who organized the meeting—the culmi-nation of years of monthly events at CUJAE campaigning to win the release of the Five.

Waters focused her remarks on the book's impact in the United States and the example the Five have set for millions around the

Havana, February 19, 2015. Cuban Five talk with students at science and engineering university. Platform, from right: Fernando González, Antonio Guerrero, René González, Professor Julián Gutiérrez, Rector Alicia Alonso, Mary-Alice Waters, editor of *Absolved by Solidarity*.

"Everything that happened isn't about us as individuals—it's about the Cuban people, who we represent."

—*Antonio Guerrero*

world being drawn into struggle by the consequences of capitalism's growing crises. Following Guerrero's initial remarks, he and his two comrades-in-arms answered questions and exchanged opinions with the audience for more than two hours.

■

Opening remarks by Antonio Guerrero

It's an honor to be here and to see the youth, the professors, the workers. During the question-and-answer period it will be Fernando's and René's turn to speak.

First, we want to thank the compañeros from Pathfinder, from the Socialist Workers Party, who day in and day out are defending socialism within the United States. We had the honor to get to know these compañeros during our years in prison, from the time our situation became known in 2001 and we began to be able to communicate.

For us Cubans it's easy to conclude that socialism is the only road possible to make this a better world. Only in a society with a different kind of mentality—like the one we've built here with so much sacrifice—can we expect the world to survive the conditions we're living through, as Fidel has alerted us more than once. In the United States it's difficult to raise consciousness about this. It's easier here in Cuba because of our history, because of the revolution and the greatness of this endeavor, which of course isn't perfect. We have many things to learn, to correct, to change—but to change within our own conditions, within our own ideals.

When I met these compañeros in person a few days ago, it felt like I had known them for many years. They supported us from the very beginning. They kept sending us magazines, books, and newspapers, in both English and Spanish. This helped us establish many relations with people inside the prisons. We began to win the admiration of other prisoners because of the support we were receiving from the outside. We passed around the books they sent us, and other prisoners would say, "This is very interesting."

Thanks to the education we received in our country, we were able to sit down and have frank discussions with anyone about any subject. "What's communism, what's socialism?" I'd often be asked. That's easy for us to explain. But we also had an important weapon—these books. They also sent us a newspaper called the *Militant* that is published in both languages. Other prisoners would get interested in reading it too.

We began to do some projects together with these compañeros. They were interested in portraying the human side of the Five, as an important way to condemn the injustice against us. One of the biggest projects we worked on was the previous book, *I Will Die the Way I've Lived*, with fifteen watercolors depicting the conditions we faced during the first seventeen months in the hole at the Federal Detention Center in Miami.

These compañeros—there's not a lot of them, they're unassuming, but they're bold in how they use their resources. They took exhibits of the watercolors to places you wouldn't imagine. And so we received letters from students, youth, children from across the United States and other countries. I remember that when the *Militant* arrived every week, it would publish the list of exhibits. It said: *I Will Die the Way I've Lived* will be shown in this city, this city, that city. The next week it said: now it will be shown here, here, and there.

From New Zealand, high school students sent me wonderful letters and photos. That too was the result of their work.

These exhibits of the watercolors about the "hole" became

a very effective weapon. The pictures attract you, they stay in your mind. And there was an explanation underneath each image.

So after they did an exhibit even in Miami, I decided to paint a new set of watercolors. Time was short. Presenting the subject of the trial was more complex. But by September 12, 2014, they already had in their hands each of the sixteen watercolors, *Absolved by Solidarity*. They were exhibited in Washington, DC.

The compañeros from Pathfinder wrote me a letter and sent me a mock-up for a new book with these watercolors. They had planned to publish it by January 1. It was already announced in the *Militant* newspaper. And then suddenly, on December 17, the three of us were back here.

We had been here for a month and a half, and we were at one event after another—I didn't even have time to ask myself what had happened with the book of watercolors. Then a few weeks ago, a compañero from the foreign ministry calls and tells me, "I have something for you that was brought by our UN ambassador. It was sent by the compañeros of Pathfinder." It was this book.

Well, I don't know how to describe how moved I was. During that brief period of time they had updated the book. You can see its quality, with photos of our return and items written by my brothers. All of it sheds light on the meaning of the title—*Absolved by Solidarity*. The solidarity, the victory won thanks to the jury of millions.

The battle doesn't end here. No battle waged by revolutionaries ends with something you once did. What you did is in the past. Are you going to live off what you did? No, you have to live from what you do each day.

Every day you have to think about the tasks, the duty we face. About your future—the future of the revolution. Your

Dear Ramon Laborino

My name is malachi maitin I am
6 years old I am sorry you are in
Jail when you are the good guy
I hope one day the FBI let you
go and you contiue to help Cuba.
Do you have kids How are you?
Do you think one day you will be
free? my counselor told me your
story I wish the best for you.

from   malachi maitin

DEAR MS. DIXON AND ALL CHILDREN OF THE
JACKIE ROBINSON COMMUNITY CENTER IN EAST
HARLEM,

I WAS VERY HAPPY TO RECEIVE YOUR BEAUTIFUL
LETTERS AND DRAWINGS AND I WOULD LIKE TO SAY
THANK YOU!!! ON BEHALF OF THE CUBAN FIVE.

WE ARE CONFIDENT THAT ONE DAY
JUSTICE WILL PREVAIL AND WE
WILL BE FREE AND IT WILL BE
THANKS TO FRIENDS LIKE YOU.

THANK YOU! I SEND YOU ♥
LOVE FROM THE CUBAN FIVE!

(MY FRIEND "CARDINAL" AND I IN PRISON)

U.S. PENITENTIARY VICTORVILLE
CALIFORNIA. JUNE 17, 2014.

FREE ALL THE CUBAN 5

Dear Gerardo Hernandez,

I know you did not commrt A
crime. I'm Angry that you Are
in Jail. My Name is Damair Jones.
I am 7 years old and in the second
Grade. I don't ha job. so I can't
pay for a good Lawyer. I hope my
letter will encourage you and
I will pray for you.

sincerly Damair Jones

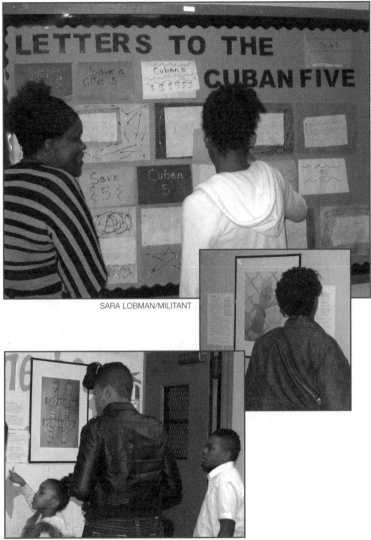

SARA LOBMAN/MILITANT

TAMAR ROSENFELD/MILITANT

Top: East Harlem, New York, May 2014. Letters written to Cuban Five by children, some 6 or 7 years old, on display at Jackie Robinson Community Center, along with exhibit of Antonio Guerrero's 15 watercolors, *I Will Die the Way I've Lived*. Children's messages conveyed both solidarity and knowledge beyond their years. **Bottom:** Viewing the exhibit. **Facing page:** Two of the letters; Gerardo's response on behalf of the Five.

LETTERS TO THE CUBAN FIVE

Save life 5

Cuban 5
5 5555 5

Save
5 5

Cuban
5

future is not just about studying and taking exams and telling people, "Look, here's my engineering diploma." It's about what that diploma represents. It's about what you have today.

When I was a student like you—I studied in the Soviet Union—I used to say, "Everything I have I owe to the revolution." And I think I've never been wrong about thinking that way.

The more selfless you are,
the happier you'll be.
You'll be better revolutionaries,
better men and women.

Times have changed. Some people in our country have started to think first and foremost about themselves. I'm not talking about you, but rather in a general sense. Selfishness has begun to reappear. I'll just tell you one thing. The more selfless you are, the happier you'll be. And you'll be better revolutionaries, better men and women. [*Applause*]

From question-and-answer period

QUESTION: Could you explain how being more selfless will make us happier?

ANTONIO: When we speak of selflessness, the first person I think of is Carlos Manuel de Céspedes.* I think of people who

---

* On October 10, 1868, Carlos Manuel de Céspedes, a wealthy Cuban landowner, freed his slaves and launched Cuba's first war for independence from Spain.

could have had everything and gave it up—even their lives—
for something more valuable than material things. This is
something you have to internalize. When they arrested us,
I thought a lot about [Cuban national hero José] Martí and
about Che [Guevara]. Everyone knows Martí could have been
whatever he wanted. Che too—he was a doctor, right? So you
begin to nourish yourself on these things.

Why were we happy while we were in prison? Well, every
morning when you get up, it's a critical moment in your life,
a new opportunity. But sometimes it's more than critical—it's
a moment when you define who you are. The more you take
the right path each day and you get up feeling useful and
with clear ideas, the more likely it is that when the decisive
moment comes you'll be better prepared.

The only way to be prepared is to have internalized this
sense of purpose, these examples, this selflessness. It has to
go beyond slogans or something you've read. It's something
inside you. And it allows you at night to rest your head on
your pillow and sleep with a tremendous peace of mind.

Let's take, for example, the situation we found ourselves
in when we were arrested in 1998. They put some guy in
front of you asking you to admit to something you didn't
do. He tells you that if you "cooperate," you can get back
all the material things you had, you'll go back to your normal life.

If not, the man tells you, "We're going to give you such a
long sentence that you're going to die in prison."

So you have to be prepared for this. You have to have already developed within you an understanding of what you
will do at such a moment. Once you pass that test and say no,
you begin to realize you're happier than those around you.
People see you and say, "Damn! Why are you laughing all the
time? Why are you so happy?"

Some of the prisoners had sold drugs and had money to own the latest model cars and other things. They suffered because they missed those things. Some had sentences of five or ten years—less than us—and they couldn't endure it. When they were released, they went back to doing the same things over again, a vicious circle. But you have a better choice—to be selfless and happy.

Today you might have all those material things, like that nice overcoat. But perhaps tomorrow you won't have it anymore.

When the Special Period began, Fidel told women something we'll never forget. He said, "Take care of that nice dress you have now, because it might have to last for a number of years." That's what he told people, right?

And there were some who said, "No, I'm going North, I'm going to look for new clothes any way I can." In exchange for what?

FERNANDO: I'm going to dare to say a few words on this subject. I agree with Tony. We human beings evolved out of the animal kingdom and have within us the instinct to fight for subsistence. But we separated from the rest of the animal kingdom. We're conscious animals, even though the instinct to be selfish remains in us.

Human society has evolved through various economic systems. Capitalism, which today is predominant, is a system that fosters selfishness in all of us.

Socialism, on the other hand, will prevail to the degree it's able to create a different culture, including the capacity to dedicate yourself to something greater than you as an individual. With all due respect to individuality, the most important thing, as José Martí said, is to do something for society, for humanity.

RENÉ: We faced some critical moments, such as the morning of September 12, 1998. Each of us had developed our own way of living. We had our loved ones. We had living conditions that in fact were better than here in Cuba, because we were working in a country that is in the heart of the imperialist world. We each had a car and a house we supposedly owned—although all of us knew that was a fallacy. History showed that later, when Olguita lost the house after my arrest. But it's true we had a comfortable life.

Suddenly, on the morning of September 12 we had to make a choice, as Antonio said. We knew that in one blow they could strip us of everything we possessed. We could have taken the other road. We knew we had to decide whether we'd betray Cuba and do whatever the prosecutor and the FBI wanted.

We chose not to betray Cuba. And from the moment they took us to the Federal Detention Center in Miami, we began to understand we would have to give up everything we had taken for granted up to that moment. All the material goods that you accumulate over years of work—the clothes, your car, the little house you fixed up.

Then came the fight to survive as human beings. The first thing they went after was our dignity—and they did so with all the force they had. Along with our happiness, as we were discussing earlier.

But gradually you realize it's possible to defend your happiness even under those conditions. That becomes part of your resistance to the blackmail, arrogance, and abuses by the prosecutors.

During the trial there were people who were even more unhappy than us prisoners—the prosecutors. We made the prosecutors the unhappiest of all the people we saw during those seven months.

When they came to court the prosecutors were the butt of

jokes by everyone, even the people in whose custody we were. They were objects of ridicule by the translator; the stenographer, Richard, who became our friend; Elizabeth, the judge's secretary; and others.

Martí said we must be cultured to be free, we must be educated to be free.

Every day of the trial—which for us began when we got up at 4:30 a.m.—was such a pleasure that when we went to sleep that night, we couldn't wait to demoralize them more the next day.

The prosecutors had everything. They would get up, I imagine, at 6:30 or 7:00 a.m. They ate whatever they wanted for breakfast. They drove to court in those sixteen-cylinder cars of theirs that guzzle half the fuel that CUJAE uses. They put on whatever clothes they wanted—the poor prosecutor had incredibly bad taste, but, well, that was her choice. [*Laughter*]

They were the most miserable-looking people you ever saw. When I publish my "diary" of the trial with Gerardo's cartoons, you'll see what I mean. Those cartoons by Gerardo circulated among the guards who escorted us, among the stenographers, among others who worked in the court.

The point is, you can learn to fight for your own happiness. Happiness is inside ourselves. The farther away you seek it, the less you will find it. [*Applause*]

QUESTION: Where did you get the strength to create art and the other things you did in prison: Antonio's paintings, Gerardo's cartoons, all the letters you sent replying to thousands of people around the world?

QUESTION: Other leaders who spent time in prison have played a historic role, like Nelson Mandela and Fidel. We're counting on you today and in the future as leaders.

QUESTION: What are some of the lessons you learned from your time in the United States?

ANTONIO: To answer the question about how we got the strength to create art in prison. Martí said we must be cultured to be free, we must be educated to be free. When we speak of culture today, we're speaking of what the revolution brought to our people. How much illiteracy was there in Cuba before the revolution? How many universities were there? Who could even think we would have something like CUJAE if there hadn't been a revolution?

I was talking with a compañero on the way here, asking about the physical state of the school. I like the hallways, so nice and clean, with all the plants. But I know there are problems here, as there are throughout the country, above all due to the economic battle we've been waging since 1990. It's been very difficult.

And I said to him, Look, the capitalists solve these things one way. In the United States they say, "I'll charge you $30,000 in tuition so you can enroll here. But since you don't have that money, you'll have to get a loan from the bank." And often you'll end up paying it off over many years. The university administrators pocket that money, and yes, you may have good air conditioning and other things. That's their system.

Who gave us what we have here in Cuba? The revolution— the workers, those who cut cane, those who work. We have something different, and you have to understand this before you start complaining or making critical comments about it. Try to go deeper, don't just stay on the surface. Get to the root of things.

When I spoke at the Lenin vocational high school here, I told students their number-one responsibility was to take care of the school and try to make it more attractive, not to criticize everything all the time. To think about how they came to have that school, where it came from.

Who gave us what we have here in Cuba? The revolution—the workers, those who cut cane, those who work.

Now, regarding the question of what gave us the strength to create art while in prison. It's rooted in the culture our people gave us, the education we received, free of charge, from the time we were children.

Anyone can write a poem. But to spend seventeen months in the hole and sixteen years in prison and create paintings that don't contain a shred of hatred or bitterness, but rather optimism, love, and freedom—that's different. That's a product of the way we were educated as revolutionaries. It's something we were able to achieve thanks to the revolution. When you find yourself behind bars, all that education and preparation helps you create.

FERNANDO: For us creativity was a form of freedom. Remember, none of us are professional artists. It came from the ability to resist, as Tony did with his paintings and his poems. As Gerardo did with his cartoons. As Ramón did with his poetry and René with his writings. Everyone in his own way. That spirit of resistance was rooted in the culture that Tony explained.

ANTONIO: A compañero here spoke about our place in history. My friend, let's not start telling a lot of stories. Just think about Che: did he do that? It's not about what someone did. It's about what you will do. Everyone is important here. Don't let anyone come here trying to be the indispensable one, the hero of the movie, OK?

That's how we see it. We even made a pact among the five of us, a commitment among brothers, that if tomorrow we see one of us with a swelled head—which won't happen—we'll tell him, "Listen, you don't seem like the person I knew." We would discuss it, because that's what you do among compañeros.

My point is, the tasks ahead are for everyone, not just of three or four people. The ones to blame for putting us in the spotlight are those who put us in jail. That's where the great struggle and solidarity came from.

Nothing that happened is about us as individuals. It's the Cuban people, who we represent. The standing we gained represents the resistance of our people. OK, it was us who this happened to. But it could just as well have happened to other compañeros we had over there.

And that's over. Now people are going to ask: So, when are you going to start working? What are your responsibilities?

We're not going to be coming back here thirty-seven more times to talk about the same things. My job can't be to come here every day and give you a *teque*.* Right now I have responsibilities to shoulder, and so do René and Fernando. We're going to work like everyone else, and work together. [*Applause*]

On the question about lessons I learned in the US. After I

---

* *Teque* is a popular Cuban term for revolutionary-sounding rhetoric rendered meaningless and mind-numbing by rote.

was arrested, the FBI went looking for people who would testify against me. They couldn't get a single person from Key
West, where I lived. They went to see people at my job. They
tried to pressure my companion Maggie—they made her go
to the FBI office endless times. They searched and searched
but found no one.

> *Our history is now in the past.*
> *We are five Cubans like any of you.*
> *We will take a place in the trenches.*
> *And, like all of you,*
> *we will be judged by the work we do.*

Just the opposite. I had a list of about twenty people I knew,
and some of them testified in my favor. There were people
who wrote to me from the first day. A woman in Key West,
the one who gave me my first job there sent me a postcard
every week.

When I was returning to Cuba I told US officials, "You're
taking away my US citizenship because Obama made that a
condition for my release. But you can't take away the affection
toward the American people that I developed." Like Martí, I
could say that I got to know the monster because I lived inside its belly. But it's not the *people* of the United States who
are the monster.

RENÉ: If I learned something in the United States, it's that
all human beings have much more in common than what
keeps us apart. US society has completely different founda-
tions from ours; that history has its consequences, just like

ours has. But when you get to know someone there, person to person, the differences tend to dissolve. What separates us is this apparatus, refined over thousands of years as a class necessity. It pits us against each other, whether by raising the banners of religion, race, or political divisions.

I don't know whether the role that we're going to play in Cuba will be a historic one. Those things are for history to decide. As Antonio said so well, our history is now in the past. We are five Cubans like any of you. We will take a place in the trenches and, like each of you, we will be judged by the work we do.

Under today's conditions, dangers are going to arise and we have to be vigilant. They will try to corrupt us and buy us off. They will try to take advantage of the problems we have. They will come in through the cracks they can open among us. They will try to create a class in Cuba—the class that fortunately we were able to kick out in 1959. They're going to try to create it here again. They're already talking about starting to encourage certain sectors of the Cuban economy and society with that in mind.

That means there will be work to do, and all of us will have to join in. Victory will be shaped more by you than by us. You are the ones who are starting your life's work under these new circumstances.

We will join in the work posed by these circumstances to the best of our ability. All we can aspire to is to be able, through our work, to live up to the standing that this episode has given us in your eyes.

As for history, I'll be happy if, when I die, my daughters are proud of me. And if any of you say I did something well, then I will have surpassed my goal. [*Applause*]

Cuban Five and Cuba's

Absolved by Solidarity
16 watercolors for 16 years of unjust imprisonment of the Cuban Five

Antonio Guerrero
In English and Spanish, bilingual edition. $15

Voices from Prison
The Cuban Five

$7. Also in Spanish, French, Arabic, and Farsi.

"I Will Die the Way I've Lived"
15 watercolors

Antonio Guerrero
$7. Also in Spanish, French, and Farsi.

The Cuban Five
Who they are
Why they were framed
Why they should be free

Articles from the socialist newsweekly the Militant

$5. Also in Spanish, French, and Farsi.

For those who want to know more about the Cuban Five—and how they came to exemplify Cuba's socialist revolution around the world—these four books are the place to start.

Socialist Revolution

Cuba and Angola
Fighting for Africa's freedom and our own

Fidel Casto, Raúl Castro, Nelson Mandela, and others

The story of Cuba's nearly 16-year internationalist mission to aid the people of Angola, in the words of those who made that history. Includes accounts by three of the Cuban Five who fought in Angola. $12. Also in Spanish.

Che Guevara Talks to Young People

Guevara challenges youth of Cuba and the world to study, to work, to become disciplined. To join the front lines of struggles, small and large. To politicize themselves and the work of their organizations. To become a different kind of human being as they strive together with working people of all lands to transform the world. $15. Also in Spanish.

Women in Cuba: The Making of a Revolution Within the Revolution
From Santiago de Cuba and the Rebel Army, to the birth of the Federation of Cuban Women

Vilma Espín, Asela de los Santos, Yolanda Ferrer

The unprecedented integration of women in the ranks and leadership of the Cuban Revolution was not an aberration. It was inseparably intertwined with the proletarian course of the leadership of the revolution from the start. This is the story of that revolution. $20. Also in Spanish.

WWW.PATHFINDERPRESS.COM

Cuba and the Coming American Revolution
Jack Barnes

This is a book about the struggles of working people in the imperialist heartland, the youth attracted to them, and the example set by the Cuban people that revolution is not only necessary—it can be made. It is about the class struggle in the US, where the political capacities and revolutionary potential of workers and farmers are today as utterly discounted by the ruling powers as were those of the Cuban toilers. And just as wrongly. $10. Also in Spanish and French.

Playa Girón/Bay of Pigs
Washington's first military defeat in the Americas

Fidel Castro, José Ramón Fernández

In fewer than 72 hours in April 1961, Cuba's revolutionary armed forces defeated a US-organized invasion by 1,500 mercenaries. The political impact of that revolutionary victory reverberated not just in Cuba but in the US and around the world. $22.
Also in Spanish.

Our History Is Still Being Written
The story of three Chinese-Cuban generals in the Cuban Revolution

Armando Choy, Gustavo Chui, and Moisés Sío Wong talk about the historic importance of Chinese immigration to Cuba, and the place of Cubans of Chinese descent in more than five decades of revolutionary action and internationalism. $20. Also in Spanish and Chinese.

from Pathfinder

Malcolm X
Black Liberation
and the Road to
Workers Power

JACK BARNES

Drawing lessons from a century and a half of struggle, this book helps us understand why it is the revolutionary conquest of power by the working class that will make possible the final battle against class exploitation and racist oppression and open the way to a world based on human solidarity. A socialist world. $20. Also in Spanish, French, Farsi and Arabic.

Cosmetics, Fashions, and the Exploitation of Women

JOSEPH HANSEN, EVELYN REED, MARY-ALICE WATERS

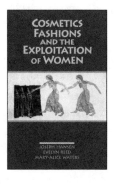

An article in 1954 in the socialist weekly the *Militant* sparked a lively debate on how the cosmetics and "fashion" industries play on the economic and emotional insecurities of women to rake in profits. Today that exchange offers a Marxist introduction to the origin of women's oppression and the struggle for liberation. $15. Also in Spanish.

The Working Class and the Transformation of Learning
The Fraud of Education Reform under Capitalism

JACK BARNES

"Until society is reorganized so that education is a human activity from the time we are very young until the time we die, there will be no education worthy of working, creating humanity." $3. Also in Spanish and French.

Capitalist 'justice'

> "Prisons of the ruling classes are not unknown territory for workers engaged in struggles. How revolutionists, communists, conduct themselves in prison, however, is always a test anew."
>
> — *from the Introduction*

Teamster Politics
FARRELL DOBBS

A central leader of the battles recorded here tells how Minneapolis Teamster Local 544 combatted FBI and other government frame-ups in the 1930s; organized the unemployed; mobilized labor opposition to US imperialism's entry into World War II; and fought to lead labor and its allies on an independent working-class political course. $19. Also in Spanish.

A Packinghouse Worker's Fight for Justice
The Mark Curtis Story
NAOMI CRAINE

The victorious eight-year battle to fight the frame-up and win freedom for Mark Curtis, a union activist and communist railroaded to prison in 1988 on charges of attempted rape and burglary. $8. Also in Spanish and French.

Socialism on Trial
Testimony at Minneapolis Sedition Trial
JAMES P. CANNON

A founding leader of American communism—facing prison for organizing working-class opposition to Washington's imperialist war preparations—uses his court testimony, as he put it, to present "patient explanations" of the Socialist Workers Party's program. $16. Also in Spanish and French.

and the US working class

50 Years of Covert Operations in the US
Washington's Political Police and the American Working Class
LARRY SEIGLE, FARRELL DOBBS, STEVE CLARK

The fight by the US working class since the late 1930s to push back expansion of Washington's political police and "national security" operations aimed at maintaining capitalist rule. And the place in that fight of the Socialist Workers Party's 15-year political campaign in the 1970s and '80s to expose federal police spying and disruption. $12. Also in Spanish.

Malcolm X Talks to Young People

Four talks and an interview given to young people in the last months of Malcolm X's life. It was as a young man behind bars, the book's introduction explains, that Malcolm began reading "whatever he could find in the prison library" and developed the "confidence in his own self-worth and discipline for hard work" that were the foundation of his later transformation into a revolutionary political leader. $15. Also in Spanish, French, and Farsi.

Letters from Prison
A Revolutionary Party Prepares for Post–WWII Labor Battles
JAMES P. CANNON

Locked up in Sandstone federal prison in 1944–45, Cannon writes to Socialist Workers Party leaders and cadres about experiences with fellow workers behind bars, reading and study during his "semester at Sandstone University," and steps to prepare the party for working-class battles that would erupt in the wake of the bloody imperialist war. $25

Also from Pathfinder

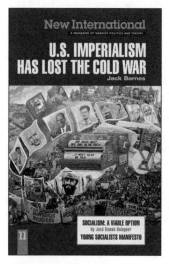

NEW INTERNATIONAL NO. 11

U.S. Imperialism Has Lost the Cold War

Jack Barnes

Contrary to imperialist expectations with the collapse of regimes across Eastern Europe and the USSR claiming to be communist, workers and farmers there have not been crushed. In today's sharpening inter-capitalist conflicts and wars, it is these toilers who will gain leadership experience as they become an intractable obstacle to imperialism's advance. $16. Also in Spanish, French, and Farsi.

The Jewish Question

A Marxist Interpretation

Abram Leon

Traces the historical rationalization of anti-Semitism to the social position of Jews as a "people-class" of merchants, moneylenders, and traders in the centuries preceding the domination of industrial capitalism. Leon explains why the propertied rulers incite Jew-hatred in the epoch of capitalism's decline. $25

The Communist Manifesto

Karl Marx, Frederick Engels

Founding document of the modern revolutionary workers movement, published in 1848. Explains why communism is not a set of preconceived principles but the line of march of the working class toward power, "springing from an existing class struggle, a historical movement going on under our very eyes." $5. Also in Spanish, French, and Farsi.

Puerto Rico: Independence Is a Necessity

Rafael Cancel Miranda

One of five Puerto Rican Nationalists imprisoned by Washington for more than 25 years until 1979 speaks out on the brutal reality of US colonial domination, the campaign to free Puerto Ricans imprisoned for their political activities, the example of Cuba's socialist revolution, and the ongoing struggle for independence. $6. Also in Spanish and Farsi.

Lenin's Final Fight

Speeches and Writings, 1922–23

In 1922 and 1923, the central leader of the world's first socialist revolution waged what was to be his last political battle. At stake was whether that revolution, and the international movement it led, would remain on the proletarian course that had brought workers and peasants to power in October 1917. $20. Also in Spanish.

The History of the Russian Revolution

Leon Trotsky

The social, economic, and political dynamics of the first socialist revolution, as told by one of its central leaders. $38. Also in Russian.

The Struggle Is My Life

Nelson Mandela

Mandela's "daily contact with the most extreme forms of repression inspired him with tireless militancy," wrote a fellow prisoner about Mandela's 27 years of confinement in the apartheid regime's maximum-security prisons. Collection includes Mandela's speeches and writings from the 1940s through his release from prison in 1990. $28

PATHFINDER AROUND THE WORLD

Visit our website for a complete list of titles and to place orders

www.pathfinderpress.com

PATHFINDER DISTRIBUTORS

UNITED STATES
(and Caribbean, Latin America, and East Asia)

> *Pathfinder Books, 227 W. 29th St., 6th Floor*
> *New York, NY 10001*

CANADA

> *Pathfinder Books, 7107 St. Denis, Suite 204*
> *Montreal, QC H2S 2S5*

UNITED KINGDOM
(and Europe, Africa, Middle East, and South Asia)

> *Pathfinder Books, 2nd Floor, 83 Kingsland High Street*
> *Dalston, London, E8 2PB*

AUSTRALIA
(and Southeast Asia and the Pacific)

> *Pathfinder, Level 1, 3/281–287 Beamish St., Campsie, NSW 2194*
> *Postal address: P.O. Box 164, Campsie, NSW 2194*

NEW ZEALAND

> *Pathfinder, 188a Onehunga Mall, Onehunga, Auckland 1061*
> *Postal address: P.O. Box 3025, Auckland 1140*